EDITOR: Maryanne Blacker

FOOD EDITOR: Pamela Clark

DESIGN DIRECTOR: Neil Carlyle

• • •

DEPUTY FOOD EDITOR: Barbara Northwood

ASSISTANT FOOD EDITORS: Jan Castorina,
Karen Green

ASSOCIATE FOOD EDITOR: Enid Morrison

CHIEF HOME ECONOMIST: Kathy Wharton

HOME ECONOMISTS: Jon Allen, Jane Ash,
Tikki Durrant, Sue Hipwell, Karen Maughan,
Voula Mantzouridis, Louise Patniotis

EDITORIAL ASSISTANT: Elizabeth Gray

KITCHEN ASSISTANT: Amy Wong

• • •

FOOD STYLISTS: Rosemary De Santis,
Carolyn Feinberg, Michelle Gorry, Jacqui Hing,
Anna Phillips, Jon Allen

PHOTOGRAPHERS: Kevin Brown, Robert Clark,
Paul Clarke, Andre Martin, Robert Taylor,
Justine Kerrigan, Georgia Moxham,
Jon Waddy

• • •

HERB CONSULTANTS: Ian & Elizabeth Hemphill

• • •

HOME LIBRARY STAFF:

ASSISTANT EDITOR: Judy Newman

ART DIRECTOR: Robbylee Phelan

CADET ARTIST: Louise McGeachie

SECRETARY: Wendy Moore

• • •

PUBLISHER: Richard Walsh

DEPUTY PUBLISHER: Graham Lawrence

• • •

Produced by The Australian Women's Weekly Home Library
Typeset by Photoset Computer Service Pty Ltd, and Letter
Perfect, Sydney. Printed by Dai Nippon Co Ltd, Tokyo, Japan
Published by Australian Consolidated Press, 54 Park Street
Sydney. Distributed by Network Distribution Company,
54 Park Street Sydney. Distributed in the U.K. by Australian
Consolidated Press (UK) Ltd (0604) 760 456. Distributed in
Canada by Whitecap Books Ltd (604) 980 9852. Distributed
in South Africa by Intermag (011) 493 3200.

© A C P 1991 (Reprint)
This publication is copyright. No part of it may be reproduced
or transmitted in any form without the written permission of
the publishers.

Cooking with Herbs.

Includes index.
ISBN 0 949892 58 0

1. Cookery (Herbs). (Series: Australian
Women's Weekly Home Library).

641.657

• • •

COVER: Clockwise from top left: Chive and Onion Twists,
Feta Cheese in Herb Oil, Oregano Herb Oil,
Minted Zucchini Ribbons, Spinach Fillo Spirals,
Venison with Fig and Chive Sauce. Table, basket, board, jug,
urn, glass canister: The Country Trader.
OPPOSITE: A selection of dried herbs. Key on page 124.
Urn, basket, chopper: The Country Trader.
BACK COVER: Clockwise from top left: Cheesy Marjoram
Bread Sticks; Sugar Snap Pea and Coriander Soup;
Gooseberry and Lemon Balm Jelly.

When you add herbs, y... ...our you can get no other way.
Fresh, wonderfully ... ...range from
pungent through to l... ...e
more you use them th... ...be
the star of a dish or support th... ...
ingredients. Some herbs in our recipes will be fa... ...hers
will be new – and that is part of the taste adventures ahead. A
bonus is that by using herbs you can eliminate or reduce salt in
your cooking. Many herbs can be dried successfully following
our two easy methods at the back of the book, and will be
handy when fresh are not available.

Pamela Clark
FOOD EDITOR

BRITISH & NORTH AMERICAN READERS: Please note that conversion charts for cup
and spoon measurements and oven temperatures are on page 126.

BASIL

Sweet basil (Ocimum basilicum) is an annual bush with curved, plump-looking veined leaves and a sweet, pungent flavour. Bush basil is smaller and has a compact shape with small pointed leaves. Basil was known in ancient Egypt, Greece and Rome, and was introduced to Europe in the 16th century. A traditional herb for pasta dishes and tomato soup, it can be chopped and used with tomato, zucchini, in salads and a variety of other dishes.

VEAL MEDALLIONS WITH HAM AND TOMATO SAUCE

Sauce can be made 4 days ahead; keep, covered, in refrigerator. Recipe unsuitable to freeze. Veal unsuitable to microwave.

8 x 80g veal medallions or steaks
1 tablespoon oil

HAM AND TOMATO SAUCE
1½ tablespoons olive oil
1 medium onion, finely chopped
1 clove garlic, crushed
60g ham, finely chopped
¼ cup dry white wine
¼ cup water
1 tablespoon tomato paste
410g can tomatoes
1 teaspoon cornflour
1 teaspoon water, extra
1 tablespoon chopped fresh basil
8 stuffed olives, sliced

Pound veal lightly. Heat oil in large frying pan, add veal in single layer, cook over medium heat until browned all over and tender. Serve with sauce.

Ham and Tomato Sauce: Heat oil in medium saucepan, add onion and garlic, stir over medium heat for about 2 minutes (or microwave on HIGH for about 3 minutes) or until onion is soft. Stir in ham, wine, water, paste and undrained crushed tomatoes, bring to

boil, reduce heat, simmer, uncovered, for 5 minutes (or microwave on HIGH for 3 minutes).

Blend cornflour with extra water in small bowl, stir into tomato mixture, stir over high heat (or microwave on HIGH for about 1 minute) until mixture boils and thickens. Stir in basil and olives just before serving.

Serves 4.

PASTA WITH BASIL SAUCE

We used fettucine pasta in this recipe. Basil sauce can be prepared a week ahead; keep, covered, in refrigerator.

This recipe is not suitable to freeze or microwave.

15g butter
⅓ cup pine nuts
1½ cups fresh basil leaves, firmly packed
2 cloves garlic, crushed
2 tablespoons grated parmesan cheese
1 teaspoon sugar
½ cup olive oil
375g pasta

Melt butter in small frying pan, add pine nuts, stir over medium heat until nuts are lightly browned; drain on absorbent paper; cool.

Process pine nuts, basil, garlic, cheese and sugar. Add oil in thin stream while motor is operating, process until combined.

Add pasta gradually to large saucepan of boiing water, boil, uncovered, until pasta is just tender, drain. Return pasta to saucepan, add basil sauce, toss gently over low heat until heated through.

Serves 4.

From left: Pasta with Basil Sauce; Veal Medallions with Ham and Tomato Sauce.

BASIL AND ZUCCHINI SOUP

Soup can be made a day ahead; keep, covered, in refrigerator. Recipe can be frozen for 2 months.

15g butter
1 tablespoon oil
1 medium onion, chopped
2 cloves garlic, crushed
6 medium zucchini, finely chopped
3 cups water
2 small chicken stock cubes, crumbled
2 teaspoons sugar
1 tablespoon lemon juice
⅓ cup chopped fresh basil

Heat butter and oil in medium saucepan, add onion and garlic, stir over medium heat for about 2 minutes (or microwave on HIGH for about 3 minutes) or until onion is soft. Stir in zucchini, water, stock cubes, sugar and juice, bring to boil, reduce heat, simmer, uncovered, for about 20 minutes (or microwave on HIGH for about 20 minutes) or until zucchini is tender, stir in basil.

Blend or process mixture in several batches until smooth, return mixture to pan; reheat. Serve topped with sour cream, paprika and extra basil leaves, if desired.

Serves 4.

LEMON BASIL SCALLOPS

Recipe best prepared close to serving time. Recipe unsuitable to freeze or microwave.

¼ cup dry white wine
2 tablespoons lemon juice
750g scallops
8 green shallots, chopped
1 clove garlic, crushed
2 teaspoons chopped fresh basil
125g unsalted butter, chopped
2 tablespoons cream

Combine wine and juice in medium frying pan, bring to boil, add scallops, reduce heat, simmer, uncovered, for about 2 minutes or until scallops are tender. Remove from pan.

Bring liquid in pan to boil, boil rapidly, uncovered, until reduced by half. Stir in shallots, garlic and basil. Remove from heat, gradually whisk in butter. Stir in cream and scallops, reheat without boiling. Serve with boiled rice, if desired.

Serves 4.

BELOW: Basil and Zucchini Soup.
RIGHT: Lemon Basil Scallops.

Below: Soup tureen: Flossoms; napkin: Appley Hoare Antiques; wheelbarrow: The Country Trader. Right: Plate and napkin: Decorator Blinds; duck ladle: Accoutrement; chair: The Itchy Palm

BOCCONCINI SALAD
WITH FRESH HERB SANDWICHES

Bocconcini cheese is fresh baby mozzarella cheese; small mozzarella can be used as a substitute. Vinaigrette can be prepared a day ahead; keep, covered, in refrigerator. Recipe unsuitable to freeze.

300g bocconcini cheese, sliced
1 radicchio lettuce
250g punnet cherry tomatoes, halved
1 cup fresh basil leaves, lightly
packed
BASIL VINAIGRETTE
½ cup oil
1 tablespoon white wine vinegar
1 tablespoon lemon juice
1 clove garlic, crushed
¼ teaspoon sugar
1 tablespoon chopped fresh basil
FRESH HERB SANDWICHES
30g butter
8 slices wholemeal bread
1 cup chopped fresh watercress
2 tablespoons chopped fresh basil

Place cheese, lettuce, tomatoes, and basil on plate; serve with vinaigrette and sandwiches.

Basil Vinaigrette: Combine all ingredients in jar; shake well.

Fresh Herb Sandwiches: Lightly butter bread, cover half the slices with combined watercress and basil; top with remaining slices. Trim crusts before cutting sandwiches.

Serves 4.

PEPPERED LAMB
WITH BASIL APPLE DRESSING

Ask your butcher to bone the loin of lamb for you. Lamb can be seasoned 2 days ahead; keep, covered, in refrigerator. Seasoned lamb can be frozen for a month. Dressing is best made just before serving. Recipe unsuitable to microwave.

750g loin of lamb, boned
1½ teaspoons cracked black
peppercorns
⅓ cup tomato paste
1 teaspoon caraway seeds
1 tablespoon oil
BASIL APPLE DRESSING
1 medium apple, chopped
½ cup fresh basil leaves, lightly
packed
1 clove garlic, crushed
½ cup cider vinegar
1 tablespoon lemon juice
½ cup oil

Remove any excess fat from lamb. Open lamb out flat, cover with plastic wrap, pound with meat mallet until lamb is an even thickness all over.

Combine peppercorns, paste and seeds in small bowl. Spread loin evenly with mixture, leaving 2cm border. Roll up loin, secure with string at 5cm intervals. Heat oil in large baking dish, add lamb, cook over high heat, turning occasionally, for about 10 minutes or until well-browned all over. Bake on rack in baking dish in moderate oven for about 30 minutes or until tender. Stand for 5 minutes before slicing. Serve with cold dressing.

ABOVE: Prawn Salad with Basil Mango Dressing. BELOW LEFT: Peppered Lamb with Basil Apple Dressing. ABOVE LEFT: Bocconcini Salad with Fresh Herb Sandwiches.

Above: Plate: Corso de Fiori; herb table and table: Duane Norris garden designers; tiles: Pazotti. Below left: Plate: Australian East India Co. Above left: Plates: Corso de Fiori; background chair and fabric: Les Olivades

Basil Apple Dressing: Blend or process apple, basil, garlic, vinegar and juice until smooth. Gradually add oil in a thin stream while motor is operating, process until thick.

Serves 4.

PRAWN SALAD WITH BASIL MANGO DRESSING

Salad and dressing are best made just before serving. This recipe is not suitable to freeze.

500g cooked king prawns
125g sugar snap peas
2 teaspoons oil
2 tablespoons pine nuts
1 radicchio lettuce
½ bunch curly endive

BASIL MANGO DRESSING
½ cup fresh basil leaves, lightly packed
1 medium mango, chopped
2 tablespoons lemon juice
¼ cup oil

Shell and devein prawns, leaving tails intact. Steam or microwave peas until just tender, drain; place in bowl of cold water, drain.

Heat oil in small saucepan, add pine nuts, stir over low heat until lightly browned; drain pine nuts on absorbent paper; cool.

Place lettuce and endive on plate, top with prawns, peas and pine nuts. Add dressing just before serving.

Basil Mango Dressing: Blend or process basil, mango and juice until smooth. Gradually add oil while motor is operating, process until combined.

Serves 4.

VEGETABLE BASIL STRUDEL

Filling can be prepared several hours ahead; keep, covered, in refrigerator. Cook strudel close to serving time. This recipe is not suitable to freeze or microwave.

60g butter
1 small eggplant, chopped
3 medium zucchini, chopped
1 medium leek, sliced
1 medium red pepper, chopped
250g baby mushrooms, sliced
2 tablespoons tomato paste
¼ cup chopped fresh basil
1 cup grated tasty cheese
8 sheets fillo pastry
60g butter, melted, extra
1 tablespoon grated parmesan
    cheese

Melt butter in large frying pan, add eggplant, zucchini, leek, pepper and mushrooms, stir over medium heat for about 5 minutes or until vegetables are soft; cool slightly. Stir in paste, basil and tasty cheese.

Layer pastry together, brushing each sheet with some of the extra butter. Place vegetable mixture along a long side of pastry, leaving 5cm border. Fold sides in, roll up like a Swiss roll. Place roll onto oven tray, brush all over with extra butter, sprinkle with parmesan cheese. Bake in moderate oven for about 25 minutes or until lightly browned.

Serves 6.

BASIL WATERMELON SORBET

You will need ¼ medium watermelon for this recipe. Sorbet can be made 2 weeks ahead; keep, covered, in freezer. Remove from freezer 20 minutes before serving. Recipe unsuitable to microwave.

1 cup sugar
1 cup water
3 cups puréed watermelon
1 tablespoon lemon juice
1 egg white
1½ tablespoons chopped fresh basil

Combine sugar and water in medium saucepan, stir over heat, without boiling, until sugar has dissolved; bring to boil, reduce heat, simmer, uncovered, without stirring, for 5 minutes; cool. Combine sugar syrup, purée and juice in large bowl. Pour mixture into 2 lamington pans, cover with foil; freeze for several hours or until firm.

Place mixture into large bowl of electric mixer or food processor with egg white, beat until creamy, stir in basil. Return mixture to pans, cover, freeze for several hours or overnight.

Serves 6.

BAY LEAVES

This thick, very slow-growing evergreen tree is popular for its decorative appearance and fragrant dark green leaves. In Roman times, laurel wreaths of bay leaves (Laurus nobilis) were used to crown heroes. Bay trees are native to the Mediterranean area and, for centuries, the leaves were used as strewing herbs because of their antiseptic qualities and fresh aroma. Bay leaves are an important ingredient of bouquet garni.

ICED CUCUMBER SOUP

Soup can be prepared 2 days ahead, keep, covered in refrigerator. Recipe unsuitable to freeze.

3 medium cucumbers, peeled, seeded
30g butter
1 medium onion, chopped
3 bay leaves
1 tablespoon plain flour
2 cups water
1 large vegetable stock cube, crumbled
½ teaspoon chopped fresh mint
2 tablespoons plain yoghurt
2 tablespoons cream

Roughly chop 2½ cucumbers. Finely chop remaining cucumber. Melt butter in medium saucepan, add onion, the 2½ cucumbers and bay leaves, stir over medium heat for about 3 minutes (or microwave on HIGH for about 4 minutes) or until onion is soft.

Stir in flour, stir over medium heat for 1 minute (or microwave on HIGH for 1 minute). Remove from heat, gradually stir in combined water and stock cube, stir over high heat (or microwave on HIGH for about 3 minutes) until mixture boils and thickens. Discard bay leaves, blend or process mixture until smooth. Stir in mint, yoghurt, cream and remaining cucumber, cover, refrigerate for several hours. Serve sprinkled with paprika, if desired.

Serves 4.

BELOW: Iced Cucumber Soup.
BELOW LEFT: Basil Watermelon Sorbet.
ABOVE LEFT: Vegetable Basil Strudel.

Above left: China, basket and herb label: Accoutrement; napkin: Appley Hoare Antiques. Below left: China: Appley Hoare Antiques; terracotta: The Itchy Palm

MARINATED PORTERHOUSE STEAKS

Porterhouse steaks are also known as New York cut steaks. Steaks can be marinated for 2 days ahead; keep, covered, in refrigerator. Recipe unsuitable to freeze or microwave.

6 porterhouse steaks
¾ cup dry red wine
2 tablespoons oil
1 tablespoon light soy sauce
1 tablespoon brown sugar
1 tablespoon seeded mustard
1 clove garlic, crushed
3 bay leaves
1 tablespoon cracked black
peppercorns

Trim excess fat from steaks. Combine remaining ingredients in large bowl, add steaks, stir to coat steaks with marinade. Cover, refrigerate for several hours or overnight.

Remove steaks from marinade, place into heated greased heavy-based large frying pan or onto heated greased barbecue plate, cook over medium heat until well browned on both sides and tender, brushing with marinade occasionally. Remove bay leaves before serving.

Serves 6.

PEPERONATA

Peperonata can be made 2 days ahead; keep, covered, in refrigerator. This recipe is not suitable to freeze or microwave.

2 medium green peppers
2 medium red peppers
½ cup olive oil
1 medium onion, sliced
2 cloves garlic, crushed
2 bay leaves
425g can tomatoes

Cut peppers in half lengthways, remove seeds and membranes. Place peppers, cut side down, on oven tray, bake in moderate oven for 20 minutes, cool slightly. Peel peppers, cut peppers into 2cm strips.

Heat oil in medium frying pan, add onion, garlic and bay leaves, stir over medium heat for about 5 minutes or until onion is soft. Add peppers and undrained crushed tomatoes to pan, bring to boil, reduce heat, cover, simmer for about 15 minutes or until peppers are soft.

Serves 4.

BELOW: Marinated Porterhouse Steaks.
RIGHT: Peperonata.

Below: Knife: The Australian East India Co; stool: Country Form. Right: Plate and bowl: Studio-Haus; chair, bread basket, board and knife: The Country Trader

BERGAMOT

Also known as bee balm, bergamot (Monarda didyma) is a perennial with oval leaves growing from a square stem. It has showy red flowers which, with the leaves, have a fragrant orange perfume. A native to North America, it was used as a tea by Oswego Indians. Following the Boston Tea Party in 1773, American settlers used it as a substitute for Indian tea. Leaves are used to flavour meat and vegetarian dishes. Flowers can be shredded and tossed over a green salad.

LAMBS' BRAINS IN CREAMY BERGAMOT SAUCE

Recipe is best made just before serving. This recipe is not suitable to freeze or microwave.

6 sets lambs' brains
plain flour
15g butter
1 tablespoon oil
2 tablespoons brandy
1 teaspoon seeded mustard
⅓ cup water
⅔ cup cream
2 tablespoons chopped fresh bergamot leaves

Place brains in bowl, cover with cold water, stand for 1 hour, drain. Peel away membrane, cut each set of brains in half. Lightly toss brains in flour, shake away excess flour.

Heat butter and oil in medium frying pan, add brains, cook over medium heat for about 3 minutes each side or until golden brown and cooked through, drain on absorbent paper.

Stir brandy into pan, stir in mustard, water and cream, bring to boil, reduce heat, simmer, uncovered, for about 10 minutes or until sauce thickens slightly. Stir in bergamot. Serve brains with sauce.

Serves 6.

TOMATO AND BERGAMOT BRIOCHES

Recipe is best prepared close to serving time. Recipe unsuitable to freeze or microwave.

7g sachet dry yeast
½ teaspoon sugar
½ cup warm water
3 cups plain flour
1 teaspoon salt
1 tablespoon sugar, extra
3 eggs, lightly beaten
155g butter, melted
1 egg yolk, lightly beaten, extra
2 tablespoons cream
TOMATO AND BERGAMOT FILLING
1 tablespoon oil
1 large onion, chopped
4 small (250g) tomatoes, peeled, chopped
½ teaspoon paprika
¼ cup chopped fresh bergamot leaves
100g hot salami, finely chopped
½ cup grated mozzarella cheese
Combine yeast, sugar, water and ¼ cup of the flour in small bowl; mix well. Cover and stand in a warm place for about 10 minutes or until foamy.

Sift remaining flour, salt and extra sugar into large bowl, make well in centre, stir in combined yeast mixture, eggs and butter; mix to a soft dough. Turn onto lightly floured surface; knead for about 3 minutes or until dough is smooth and elastic. Place into a large oiled bowl, cover with plastic wrap, stand in warm place for about 1 hour or until dough is doubled in size.

Knead dough for 5 minutes until smooth and elastic. Divide dough into 12 equal portions. Remove a quarter of the dough from each portion. Flatten larger portions into rounds approximately 10cm in diameter. Top each round with 1 level tablespoon filling, pinch edges together around filling to seal, place sealed side down in 12 greased small brioche moulds (½ cup capacity). Shape smaller portions of dough into rounds.

Brush dough in moulds with combined extra egg yolk and cream. Place small rounds on top. Push a wooden skewer through centre of small round to base of mould; remove skewer. Brush with remaining egg yolk and cream, stand in a warm place for about 15 minutes or until brioches are doubled in size. Bake in a moderate oven for about 15 minutes or until well risen and golden.

Tomato and Bergamot Filling: Heat oil in medium frying pan, add onion, stir over medium heat for about 2 minutes or until onion is soft. Stir in tomatoes and paprika, bring to boil, reduce heat, simmer, uncovered, for about 3 minutes or until reduced and thickened. Stir in bergamot and salami, stir over medium heat for about 2 minutes or until all liquid has evaporated. Remove from heat, cool slightly; stir in cheese.

Makes 12.

BELOW: Tomato and Bergamot Brioches.

Below: Plate: The Country Trader.

LEFT: Lambs' Brains in Creamy Bergamot Sauce.

Left: Plates: Noritake

BORAGE

A particularly attractive herb with vivid blue, star-shaped flowers, borage (Borago officinalis) has large cucumber-flavoured rough leaves, covered in fine bristly hairs. Native to the Middle East, it grows easily wherever cultivated. It is said that borage makes people merry and eases melancholy, probably because it was often used in alcoholic drinks! The flowers can be crystallised and used to garnish desserts. Use the leaves in soups and salads of various types.

BORAGE WINE CUP

Recipe is best made just before serving. Recipe unsuitable to freeze.

½ cup brandy
2 tablespoons castor sugar
750ml bottle dry white wine
½ cup orange juice
1 cup crushed ice
750ml bottle pink champagne
300ml can lemonade
300ml can ginger ale
2 tablespoons chopped fresh
   borage leaves

Blend brandy, sugar, wine, juice and ice until combined. Combine champagne, lemonade, ginger ale, borage and wine mixture in large bowl just before serving.
   Makes about 2¼ litres (9 cups).

TROPICAL FRUIT SALAD WITH LIME SYRUP

You need 4 limes for this recipe. Recipe can be made a day ahead; keep, covered, in refrigerator. Recipe unsuitable to freeze or microwave.

3 passionfruit
2 medium kiwi fruit, chopped
1 small pineapple, chopped
250g punnet strawberries, chopped
1 small rockmelon, chopped
1 small papaw, chopped
LIME SYRUP
½ cup lime juice
½ cup sugar
2 tablespoons chopped fresh
   borage leaves

Combine passionfruit pulp and remaining fruit in large bowl. Add lime syrup, toss gently to combine, cover, refrigerate for several hours.
Lime Syrup: Combine juice and sugar in small saucepan, stir over heat without boiling, until sugar has dissolved. Bring to boil, reduce heat, simmer, uncovered, without stirring, for 5 minutes; cool. Stir in borage.
   Serves 6.

LEFT: Borage Wine Cup. RIGHT: Tropical Fruit Salad with Lime Syrup.

Left: Bottle and glasses: Accoutrement. Right: Bowl: Accoutrement; spoon and jug: Appley Hoare Antiques; lace: Laura Ashley

CARAWAY

Caraway (Carum carvi) has delicate frond-like leaves and bursts of small white flowers from which the fragrant brown anise-flavoured seeds are gathered. Julius Caesar's bread contained caraway seeds, which were also used in ancient times to freshen the breath. Chopped leaves and seeds can be used in many savoury dishes, and in delicious breads, biscuits and cakes.

CARAWAY WATER BISCUITS

Biscuits can be made a week ahead; keep in airtight container. Biscuits can be frozen for 2 months. Recipe unsuitable to microwave.

1½ cups plain flour
½ cup self-raising flour
60g butter
1 tablespoon caraway seeds
2 teaspoons chopped fresh
    caraway leaves
2 tablespoons grated fresh
    parmesan cheese
½ cup water, approximately

Sift flours into medium bowl, rub in butter. Stir in caraway seeds, caraway leaves and cheese. Make well in centre, add enough water to mix to a firm dough. Turn onto lightly floured surface, knead lightly until smooth, roll dough out thinly on lightly floured surface until 2mm thick.

Prick all over with fork. Cut out biscuits using 2cm cutter. Place on lightly greased oven trays, bake in moderate oven for about 12 minutes or until lightly browned; cool biscuits on wire racks.

Makes about 80.

Right: Plate and basket: The Country Trader

LEEK AND CARAWAY FLANS

If fresh caraway leaves are unavailable, parsley can be substituted. Flan cases can be made a day ahead; keep in airtight container or freeze for 2 months. Flans unsuitable to freeze or microwave.

125g packet cream cheese
125g butter
1¼ cups plain flour
1 teaspoon caraway seeds
30g butter, extra
1 medium leek, thinly sliced
1 small red pepper, finely chopped
⅔ cup grated fresh parmesan cheese
1 cup milk
3 eggs, lightly beaten
1 tablespoon chopped fresh
    caraway leaves

Beat cream cheese and butter in small bowl with electric mixer until light and creamy. Stir in sifted flour and caraway seeds, mix to a soft dough. Turn dough onto lightly floured board, knead lightly until smooth, cover, refrigerate for 15 minutes. Roll dough between 2 sheets of plastic wrap or greaseproof paper until large enough to line 6 x 9cm deep flan tins; trim edges, refrigerate further 15 minutes.

Cover flan cases with greaseproof paper, fill with dried beans or rice. Bake on tray in moderate oven for 7 minutes, remove paper and beans, bake 7 minutes or until golden brown.

Melt extra butter in small frying pan, add leek and pepper, stir over high heat (or microwave on HIGH for about 3 minutes) until leek is tender. Spoon leek mixture evenly into flan cases, sprinkle with cheese. Combine milk, eggs and caraway leaves in jug, pour over cheese. Bake in moderate oven for about 20 minutes or until set.

Makes 6.

LEFT: Caraway Water Biscuits.
RIGHT: Leek and Caraway Flans.

BAKED PASTA WITH CARAWAY AND CHILLI

We made our own pasta for this recipe but any fresh or dried pasta can be used. You need to buy 250g fresh pasta or 150g dried pasta. Recipe is best made close to serving time. This recipe is not suitable to freeze or microwave.

1 cup plain flour
1 egg
1 tablespoon oil
1½ cups milk
2 small chicken stock cubes, crumbled
3 eggs, lightly beaten, extra
250g ricotta cheese
2 tablespoons grated fresh parmesan cheese
1 tablespoon chopped fresh caraway leaves
1 small fresh red chilli, chopped
¼ teaspoon cracked black peppercorns

Lightly grease large shallow ovenproof dish (6 cup capacity).

Process flour, egg and oil until combined. Turn dough onto lightly floured surface, knead for about 5 minutes or until smooth. Make pasta following your machine's directions.

Add pasta gradually to large saucepan of boiling water, boil, uncovered, until just tender; drain.

Combine remaining ingredients in large bowl, add pasta, mix well. Spoon into prepared dish. Bake in moderate oven for about 1¼ hours, or until set, stand for 5 minutes before serving.

Serves 4.

RIGHT: Baked Pasta with Caraway and Chilli.

FRIED CAMEMBERT WITH PLUM SAUCE

You can substitute 2 x 250g packets camembert cheese, if preferred. Cheese can be coated a day ahead; keep, covered, in refrigerator. Cook cheese just before serving. Recipe unsuitable to freeze or microwave.

500g packet camembert cheese
¼ cup chopped fresh caraway leaves
½ teaspoon caraway seeds
plain flour
2 eggs, lightly beaten
¼ cup milk
1 cup packaged breadcrumbs
oil for deep-frying

PLUM SAUCE
425g can satsuma plums
1 tablespoon lemon juice
1 tablespoon green ginger wine
2 teaspoons light soy sauce

Cut camembert into 16 wedges, press cut sides with combined caraway leaves and seeds, toss in flour, shake off excess flour. Dip wedges in combined eggs and milk, then in breadcrumbs. Place wedges on tray, refrigerate for 10 minutes. Dip wedges into egg mixture again, then in breadcrumbs. Refrigerate further 10 minutes. Deep-fry in hot oil until golden brown; drain on absorbent paper. Serve with warm plum sauce.

Plum Sauce: Drain plums, reserve syrup. Remove seeds from plums. Blend or process plums and reserved syrup until smooth, strain. Pour mixture into small saucepan, stir in juice, wine and sauce, bring to boil, remove from heat.

Makes 16.

GRILLED QUAIL
IN CARAWAY MARINADE

Quail and lettuce are best cooked just before serving. This recipe is not suitable to freeze or microwave.

6 quail
⅓ cup lemon juice
2 tablespoons oil
⅓ cup chopped fresh caraway leaves
2 teaspoons caraway seeds
1 teaspoon ground cumin
1 tablespoon honey
BRAISED LETTUCE
15g butter
1 small clove garlic, crushed
1 medium red pepper, sliced
1 large iceberg lettuce, shredded

Using sharp scissors or knife, cut down both sides of backbone of quail. Remove and discard backbones. Use heel of hand to press quail flat; tuck wings under bodies.

Combine juice, oil, caraway leaves, seeds, cumin and honey in medium bowl, add quail, stir gently to coat quail with marinade; refrigerate overnight. Grill or barbecue quail for about 5 minutes on each side or until cooked as desired, brushing with marinade during cooking. Serve quail with braised lettuce.

Braised Lettuce: Heat butter in large frying pan, add garlic and pepper, stir over medium heat for about 2 minutes or until pepper is soft. Stir in lettuce,

toss over medium heat for about 40 seconds or until lettuce is just wilted.

Serves 6.

ABOVE: Grilled Quail in Caraway Marinade.
LEFT: Fried Camembert with Plum Sauce.

Above: Plate and decanter: Flossoms

CHERVIL

Sometimes referred to as "gourmet's parsley", chervil (Anthriscus cerefolium) is a small biennial herb with soft, ferny, bright green leaves similar in appearance to parsley and tasting slightly of aniseed and pepper. Chervil was used as a food by the Syrians and Pliny wrote of it being used as a seasoning and a cure for hiccoughs in the first century AD. Add to cooking only for the last 5 to 10 minutes in order to keep its delicate flavour. Chervil enhances eggs, salads, poultry, fish, soups and mornays, among many dishes.

SPINACH AND CHERVIL SOUP

We used old potatoes for this recipe. Soup can be made a day ahead; keep, covered, in refrigerator. Recipe unsuitable to freeze.

30g butter
2 medium onions, chopped
500g potatoes, chopped
1¾ litres (7 cups) water
2 small chicken stock cubes, crumbled
1 cup fresh chervil leaves
10 large (¼ bunch) English spinach leaves, chopped
½ cup cream

Melt butter in large saucepan, add onions, stir over medium heat for about 3 minutes (or microwave on HIGH for about 4 minutes) or until onions are soft. Stir in potatoes, stir over medium heat for 3 minutes (or microwave on HIGH for 3 minutes). Stir in water and stock cubes, bring to boil, reduce heat, cover, simmer for about 20 minutes (or microwave on HIGH for about 15 minutes) or until potatoes are soft.

Stir in chervil and spinach, simmer further 5 minutes (or microwave on HIGH for 3 minutes). Blend or process mixture in several batches until smooth. Return to saucepan, stir in cream, reheat mixture without boiling.

Serves 6.

LEFT: Spinach and Chervil Soup.
RIGHT: Farmhouse Chicken Pie.

Left: Soup tureen: Villeroy & Boch

FARMHOUSE CHICKEN PIE

Pie is best baked just before serving. Filling for pie can be made 2 days ahead; keep, covered, in refrigerator. Pie unsuitable to freeze or microwave.

4 chicken breast fillets
1 litre (4 cups) water
¼ cup dry white wine
2 small chicken stock cubes, crumbled
1 medium onion, chopped
1 stick celery, chopped
1 bay leaf
1 egg, lightly beaten
375g packet frozen puff pastry
CREAMY VEGETABLE FILLING
2 medium carrots, chopped
1 cup fresh or frozen peas
60g butter
1 medium onion, sliced
⅓ cup plain flour
½ cup cream

1 egg, lightly beaten
⅓ cup chopped fresh chervil
440g can corn kernels, drained

Place chicken in medium frying pan, pour in enough of the water to cover, add wine, stock cubes, onion, celery and bay leaf. Bring to boil, reduce heat, cover, simmer gently for about 10 minutes (or microwave on HIGH for about 6 minutes) or until chicken is just cooked through. Remove chicken from stock, cool. Bring stock to boil, boil for 10 minutes, strain; reserve 1 cup stock for filling.

Chop chicken roughly, add to filling; mix well. Spoon filling into deep 20cm pie dish. Brush edge of pie dish with egg. Roll pastry out on lightly floured surface to fit top of pie dish, trim edges, press edges firmly to seal, decorate with remaining pastry, if desired. Brush with egg.

Bake in moderately hot oven for 10 minutes, reduce heat to moderate,

bake further 20 minutes or until golden.

Creamy Vegetable Filling: Boil, steam or microwave carrots and peas until tender; drain. Melt butter in medium saucepan, add onion, stir over medium heat for about 2 minutes (or microwave on HIGH for about 3 minutes) or until onion is soft. Stir in flour, stir over medium heat for 2 minutes (or microwave on HIGH for 2 minutes). Remove from heat, gradually stir in combined reserved stock and cream. Stir over high heat (or microwave in HIGH for about 3 minutes) until mixture boils and thickens. Stir carrots and peas into sauce with egg, chervil and corn.

Serves 6

ROAST VEAL ROLL WITH CHERVIL

Ask your butcher to pound the veal fillet into 1 large, thin steak. Recipe unsuitable to freeze or microwave.

100g sliced prosciutto
750g veal fillet, pounded
1 cup grated mozzarella cheese
¼ cup grated fresh parmesan cheese
¼ cup roasted unsalted cashew nuts, chopped
⅔ cup stale breadcrumbs
¼ cup chopped fresh chervil
1 clove garlic, crushed
¼ cup plain flour
2 tablespoons oil
2 tablespoons plain flour, extra
½ cup dry white wine
½ cup water
1 small beef stock cube, crumbled

Lay prosciutto slices over veal. Combine cheeses, nuts and breadcrumbs in medium bowl; mix well. Spread cheese mixture over prosciutto, leaving 2cm border. Combine chervil and garlic in small bowl, sprinkle over cheese mixture. Fold in short sides of veal, roll up from long side, secure with string at 5cm intervals. Roll veal in flour, shake away excess flour.

Heat oil in baking dish, add veal, cook over high heat, turning occasionally, until browned all over. Bake, uncovered, in moderately hot oven for about 40 minutes or until tender.

Remove veal from dish; cover, keep warm in oven. Drain juices from dish, leaving about 2 tablespoons of juice in dish.

Place dish over heat, stir in extra flour, stir over medium heat until browned. Remove from heat, gradually stir in wine and combined water and stock cube, stir over high heat until mixture boils and thickens. Pour sauce over sliced veal before serving.

Serves 6.

GOATS' MILK CHEESE QUICHE

Pastry case can be made a week ahead; keep in airtight container. Completed quiche unsuitable to freeze or microwave.

PASTRY
1¾ cups plain flour
125g butter
1 egg yolk, lightly beaten
2 teaspoons orange juice, approximately
FILLING
200g goats' milk cheese
2 bacon rashers, chopped
1 spring onion, chopped
½ cup chopped fresh chervil
4 eggs, lightly beaten
300ml carton cream
⅓ cup milk
½ cup grated tasty cheese
¼ cup stale breadcrumbs

Pastry: Sift flour into medium bowl, rub in butter. Add egg yolk and enough juice to make ingredients cling together. Knead pastry gently on lightly floured surface until smooth; cover, refrigerate for 30 minutes. Roll pastry large enough to line deep 23cm flan tin; lift pastry into flan tin, gently ease pastry into side of tin; trim edge.

Place tin on oven tray, cover pastry with greaseproof or baking paper, fill

with dried beans or rice. Bake in moderately hot oven for 10 minutes, remove paper and beans, bake further 7 minutes or until lightly browned; cool to room temperature.

Sprinkle goats' milk cheese over pastry, pour remaining filling mixture over cheese. Bake in moderate oven for about 40 minutes or until filling is set and lightly browned. Stand quiche for 5 minutes before serving.

Filling: Crumble goats' milk cheese coarsely. Stir bacon in small frying pan over medium heat for about 3 minutes or until browned. Add onion, stir over medium heat for about 2 minutes or until onion is soft. Drain on absorbent paper; cool. Combine bacon mixture, chervil, eggs, cream, milk, tasty cheese and breadcrumbs in medium bowl; mix well.

Serves 6.

ABOVE: Goats' Milk Cheese Quiche.
ABOVE LEFT: Roast Veal Roll with Chervil.

Above left: Platter: The Country Trader; column: Australian East India Co. Above: plate: Villa Italiana

CHEESE AND CHERVIL SOUFFLES

Recipe is best made just before serving. Soufflés unsuitable to freeze or microwave.

125g butter
⅓ cup plain flour
1 cup milk
1 cup grated tasty cheese
¼ cup chopped fresh chervil
4 eggs, separated
1 egg white, extra

Melt butter in medium saucepan (or microwave on HIGH for 1 minute), stir in flour, stir over medium heat for 1 minute (or microwave on HIGH for 1 minute). Remove from heat, gradually stir in milk, stir over high heat (or microwave on HIGH for about 3 minutes) until mixture boils and thickens. Stir in cheese and chervil, stir until the cheese melts (sauce will appear curdled at this stage).

Transfer mixture to large bowl, quickly stir in egg yolks. Beat all egg whites in small bowl until firm peaks form, fold into mixture in 2 batches. Spoon mixture evenly into 6 soufflé dishes (½ cup capacity), place on oven tray. Bake in moderately hot oven for about 20 minutes or until golden brown.

Makes 6.

CHERVIL MUSTARD SAUCE

Sauce is suitable to serve with chicken, veal or fish. Sauce can be made a day ahead; keep, covered, in refrigerator. Recipe unsuitable to freeze or microwave.

1 cup water
1 small chicken stock cube, crumbled
1 tablespoon French mustard
2 teaspoons lemon juice
2 teaspoons cornflour
1 tablespoon water, extra
¼ cup thickened cream
2 tablespoons chopped fresh chervil

Combine water, stock cube, mustard and juice in medium saucepan, bring to boil, reduce heat, simmer, uncovered, for about 5 minutes or until reduced by one-third. Blend cornflour with water, stir into mixture with cream, stir over high heat until mixture boils and thickens. Stir in chervil before serving.

Makes about 1 cup.

TOP LEFT: Cheese and Chervil Soufflés.
LEFT: Chervil Mustard Sauce.

Top left: Basket: Flossoms. Left: Bowl and whisk: The Bay Tree; wooden bowl and table: The Country Trader

CHICORY

Also known as Belgian endive, witlof and succory, chicory (Cichorum intybus) is a perennial herb with long leaves like English spinach. Flowers that close at midday cluster on long stalks like blue dandelions. The early Greeks and Romans cooked chicory as a vegetable. In ancient times it was used in love potions and by Arabian physicians. The roasted ground root is a well-known additive or substitute for coffee in Europe. Use the blanched young tender leaves as a salad vegetable.

CHICORY, GARLIC AND LEMON DRESSING

Dressing is best made on day of serving. Recipe unsuitable to freeze.

1 teaspoon grated lemon rind
1 tablespoon lemon juice
2 egg yolks
1 teaspoon seeded mustard
1 clove garlic, crushed
⅔ cup olive oil
¼ teaspoon sugar
¼ cup chopped fresh chicory

Blend or process rind, juice, egg yolks, mustard and garlic until smooth. With motor operating, gradually add oil in a thin stream, process until mixture thickens. Add sugar and chicory, process until smooth. Serve sauce at room temperature with avocado and mango or fruits of your choice.

RIGHT: Chicory, Garlic and Lemon Dressing.

Right: Plate: Villeroy & Boch

CHICKEN AND CHICORY CASSEROLE

Casserole is best made close to serving time. This recipe is not suitable to freeze.

750g chicken thigh fillets, halved
plain flour
30g butter
2 tablespoons oil
1 medium onion, sliced
1 clove garlic, crushed
1 large carrot, sliced
⅓ cup dry sherry
1½ tablespoons plain flour, extra
1 cup water
2 tablespoons sour cream
¼ cup chopped fresh chicory

Toss chicken in flour; shake away excess flour. Heat butter and oil in heatproof dish, add chicken in single layer. Cook chicken over medium heat, turning often, until browned all over; remove chicken from dish.

Add onion and garlic to dish, stir over medium heat for about 2 minutes (or microwave on HIGH for about 3 minutes) or until onion is soft. Return chicken to dish with carrot and sherry. Blend extra flour with water, stir into chicken mixture, cover, bake in moderate oven for about 1 hour (or microwave on HIGH for about 20 minutes) or until chicken is tender. Stir sour cream and chicory into chicken mixture just before serving.

Serves 4.

CHICORY PAKORAS WITH MINTED COCONUT CHUTNEY

Pakoras are best made close to serving time. Chutney can be made 2 days ahead; keep, covered, in refrigerator. Pakoras are unsuitable to freeze or microwave.

2 medium potatoes, finely chopped
1 medium leek, finely chopped
250g broccoli, finely chopped
2 medium carrots, finely chopped
1 cup fresh or frozen peas
2 tablespoons chopped fresh chicory
1 cup chick pea flour
⅓ cup self-raising flour
1 teaspoon garam masala
1½ teaspoons ground coriander
1 teaspoon ground cumin
1 egg, lightly beaten
1¼ cups water
oil for deep-frying
MINTED COCONUT CHUTNEY
1 cup coconut
1 small fresh red chilli, finely chopped
¼ cup plain yoghurt
¼ cup orange juice
1 tablespoon chopped fresh chicory
2 teaspoons chopped fresh mint
¼ cup water

Boil, steam or microwave vegetables until soft, drain well; cool. Combine vegetables and chicory in medium bowl; mix well.

Sift flours and spices into large bowl, make well in centre, gradually stir in combined egg and water, mix to a smooth batter (or blend or process ingredients until smooth). Cover, stand

for 30 minutes to thicken slightly.

Stir vegetable mixture into batter. Deep-fry heaped tablespoons of pakora mixture in hot oil until golden brown and cooked through; drain on absorbent paper. Serve warm pakoras with chutney.

Minted Coconut Chutney: Blend or process all ingredients until smooth.

Serves 6 as an entree.

ABOVE LEFT: Chicken and Chicory Casserole.
ABOVE: Chicory Pakoras with Minted Coconut Chutney.

Above left: Casserole dish: Australian East India Co.

LAMB WELLINGTON

Ask the butcher to bone the lamb loins for you. Recipe can be prepared a day ahead; bake on day of serving. This recipe is not suitable to freeze or microwave.

2 x 500g boned loins of lamb
2 tablespoons oil
375g packet frozen puff pastry,
    thawed
1 egg, lightly beaten
CHICORY AND MUSHROOM FILLING
30g butter
1 medium onion, finely chopped
1 clove garlic, crushed
250g mushrooms, finely chopped
½ cup chopped fresh chicory
1½ tablespoons plain flour
¼ cup madeira
½ cup stale breadcrumbs
MADEIRA SAUCE
1½ tablespoons plain flour
1⅓ cups water
1 small beef stock cube, crumbled
¼ cup madeira
½ teaspoon French mustard
2 teaspoons Worcestershire sauce

Remove any excess fat and skin from lamb; roll up tightly and secure rolls with string at 5cm intervals.

Heat oil in large frying pan, add lamb, cook over high heat, turning often, until browned all over. Reduce heat to medium, cook further 15 minutes or until almost cooked through. Remove from heat, reserve 2 tablespoons pan juices for sauce. Cool meat to room temperature; remove string.

Cut pastry in half crossways. Roll half into a rectangle large enough to encase 1 loin of lamb. Spread half the filling over pastry, leaving 2cm border. Place loin in centre of pastry, brush edges lightly with egg. Fold short sides of pastry in, fold long sides over lamb, press seam to seal. Place seam-side down on oven tray, brush all over with egg. Repeat with remaining pastry, filling and loin of lamb.

Bake in very hot oven for 10 minutes, reduce heat to moderate, bake further 20 minutes or until pastry is puffed and golden brown. Serve sliced with sauce.

Chicory and Mushroom Filling: Melt butter in medium frying pan, add onion and garlic, stir over medium heat for about 2 minutes (or microwave on HIGH for about 3 minutes) or until onion is soft. Add mushrooms and chicory, stir over medium heat for further 2 minutes (or microwave on HIGH for 2 minutes).

Stir in flour, stir over medium heat for 1 minute (or microwave on HIGH for 1 minute). Remove from heat, gradually stir in madeira, stir over high heat (or microwave on HIGH for about 1 minute) until mixture boils and thickens. Remove from heat, stir in breadcrumbs; cool mixture to room temperature.

Madeira Sauce: Heat reserved pan juices in medium saucepan, stir in flour, stir over medium heat for about 2 minutes (or microwave on HIGH for about 2 minutes) or until golden brown. Remove from heat, gradually stir in combined water, stock cube, madeira, mustard and sauce. Stir over high heat (or microwave on HIGH for about 3 minutes) until mixture boils and thickens. Reduce heat, simmer for 2 minutes (or microwave on HIGH for 1 minute); strain.

Serves 6 to 8.

RIGHT: Lamb Wellington.

RIGHT: Plate: The Country Trader; cupboard: Country Form

CHIVES

There are two varieties of chives (Allium schoenoprasum). Onion chives resemble a clump of fine grass when young, and mature to become tubular with mauve flowers. Garlic chives have flat leaves like blades of grass, small white flowers and a mild garlic flavour. In 3000 BC, the Chinese are said to have used chives, and in AD 812 the Emperor Charlemagne listed them among the 70 herbs in his garden. Use chives in many dishes for colour and flavour.

SALMON AND CHIVE PATE

Pâté can be made a day ahead; keep, covered, in refrigerator. Recipe unsuitable to freeze or microwave.

220g can salmon, drained
125g packaged cream cheese,
    softened
½ cup mayonnaise
2 tablespoons lemon juice
125g butter, melted
2 tablespoons chopped fresh chives

Blend or process salmon, cream cheese, mayonnaise and juice until well combined. Gradually add butter, while motor is operating; blend or process until smooth. Stir in chives. Pour mixture into serving dish. Refrigerate pâté until set.
    Makes 2 cups.

BUTTERFLY PRAWNS WITH CHIVE AND GINGER SAUCE

Prawns can be filled a day ahead; keep, covered, in refrigerator. Recipe unsuitable to freeze or microwave.

18 medium uncooked king prawns
1 tablespoon oil
15g butter
PRAWN FILLING
8 medium (400g) uncooked king
    prawns, shelled
½ cup cream
CHIVE AND GINGER SAUCE
2 teaspoons butter
¼ cup chopped fresh chives
2 teaspoons grated fresh ginger
1 tablespoon dry white wine
1 cup cream
½ teaspoon cornflour
1 tablespoon water
¼ large vegetable stock cube,
    crumbled
2 teaspoons chopped fresh chives,
    extra

Shell prawns, leaving tails intact. Cut almost through backs of prawns, remove dark veins. Press prawns open gently along cut side with knife. Spoon prawn filling into piping bag fitted with star tube. Pipe small amount of filling onto uncut side of each prawn. Press tail gently onto filling. Refrigerate for 10 minutes.

Heat oil and butter in medium frying pan, add prawns, cover, cook over medium heat for about 5 minutes or until prawns are cooked through. Serve with sauce.

Prawn Filling: Blend or process prawns until smooth. Add cream, mix until just combined. Refrigerate for 10 minutes before using.

Chive and Ginger Sauce: Melt butter in small saucepan, add chives and ginger, stir over medium heat for 1 minute. Stir in wine and cream, bring to boil, reduce heat, simmer, uncovered, for 2 minutes. Blend cornflour with water and stock cube, stir into pan, stir over high heat until mixture boils and thickens. Strain sauce; stir in extra chives.

Serves 6.

ABOVE: Butterfly Prawns with Chive and Ginger Sauce. LEFT: Salmon and Chive Pâté.

Above: Plate: Made in Japan. Left: Chair, bowl and basket: Flossoms

FIVE HERB SAUCE

Sauce can be served with cold meat or vegetables. Sauce can be made a day ahead; keep, covered, in refrigerator. This recipe is unsuitable to freeze or microwave.

2 hard-boiled eggs
2 tablespoons lime juice
1 cup sour cream
2 tablespoons milk
1 small onion, chopped
¼ cup chopped fresh chives
2 teaspoons chopped fresh dill
2 teaspoons chopped fresh parsley
2 teaspoons chopped fresh oregano
2 teaspoons chopped fresh mint

Chop egg whites and reserve. Push egg yolks through fine sieve into medium bowl, stir in juice; mix to a smooth paste. Stir in sour cream, milk, onion, herbs and reserved egg whites.

Makes about 1½ cups.

CHIVE AND BACON OMELETTE

Recipe is best made just before serving. This recipe is not suitable to freeze or microwave.

4 eggs
2 tablespoons water
1 tablespoon chopped fresh chives
15g butter
FILLING
4 bacon rashers, chopped
125g baby mushrooms, sliced
½ medium red pepper, sliced
1 tablespoon chopped fresh chives

Whisk eggs and water in medium bowl until just combined, stir in chives. Melt half the butter in medium frying pan, pour in half the egg mixture, cover, cook over medium heat until omelette is almost set and lightly browned underneath. Spoon half the filling over half the omelette, fold omelette over filling, slide onto plate.

Repeat with remaining butter, egg mixture and filling.

Filling: Cook bacon in medium frying pan over high heat for 3 minutes, add mushrooms, pepper and chives, stir over medium heat for about 2 minutes or until mushrooms are soft.

Serves 2.

CHIVE AND ONION TWISTS

Twists are at their best freshly cooked and served warm. Recipe unsuitable to freeze; twists unsuitable to microwave.

15g butter
1 medium onion, finely chopped
½ cup chopped fresh chives
2 sheets ready-rolled puff pastry
1 tablespoon milk
½ cup grated tasty cheese

Melt butter in small saucepan, add onion, stir over medium heat for about 2 minutes (or microwave on HIGH for about 3 minutes) or until onion is soft.

Drain onion on absorbent paper; cool. Combine onion and chives in medium bowl. Spread onion mixture evenly over 1 sheet of pastry. Cover with remaining pastry. Brush with milk, sprinkle with cheese.

Cut pastry into 2cm wide strips. Twist strips, place onto greased oven trays; brush lightly with milk. Bake in hot oven for about 8 minutes or until golden brown. Cool on wire racks.

Makes 12.

ABOVE LEFT: From top: Five Herb Sauce; Chive and Bacon Omelette. FAR LEFT: Chive and Onion Twists.

Above left: Background screen, basket and table: Corso de Fiori; frying pan: Made Where

35

CHICKEN, CHIVE AND PINEAPPLE POCKETS

Filling can be made 2 days ahead; keep, covered, in refrigerator. Recipe unsuitable to freeze or microwave.

4 chicken breast fillets
2 teaspoons cornflour
1 tablespoon sesame seeds
2 tablespoons oil
1 teaspoon curry powder
150ml can coconut cream
2 green shallots, sliced
450g can pineapple pieces, drained
¼ cup sour cream
2 tablespoons chopped fresh chives
4 pita pocket breads

Cut chicken into 2cm pieces. Dust lightly with combined cornflour and sesame seeds. Heat half the oil in large frying pan, add half the chicken, stir over medium heat until chicken is just cooked, drain on absorbent paper. Repeat with remaining oil and chicken; drain on absorbent paper.

Return chicken to pan, add curry powder, stir over medium heat for 1 minute. Stir in coconut cream, bring to boil, reduce heat, simmer for 1 minute or until thickened. Remove from heat, stir in shallots, pineapple and sour cream. Refrigerate mixture until cold, stir in chives. Cut each pocket bread in half, fill with mixture.

Serves 4.

ABOVE: Venison with Fig and Chive Sauce. BELOW: Chicken, Chive and Pineapple Pockets.

Above: Plate: Flossoms; table: Nice and Old. Below: plate: Made Where

VENISON WITH FIG AND CHIVE SAUCE

Venison is available from specialty game shops. Recipe is best prepared just before serving. Recipe unsuitable to freeze or microwave.

1 tablespoon oil
600g piece venison leg steak
2 green shallots, chopped
2 teaspoons plain flour
½ cup dry red wine
½ cup water
¼ large vegetable stock cube, crumbled
1 teaspoon grated lemon rind
2 teaspoons honey
2 teaspoons butter
2 tablespoons chopped fresh chives
2 medium fresh figs

Heat oil in small baking dish, add venison, cook over high heat for 2 minutes on each side to seal. Bake in moderate oven for about 20 minutes or until cooked as desired. Transfer to plate, cover, keep warm while preparing sauce.

Drain juices from dish, leaving about 2 teaspoons juices in dish. Heat juices in dish, add shallots, stir over medium heat for about 1 minute or until shallots are soft. Stir in flour, stir over medium heat for about 1 minute or until golden brown. Remove from heat, gradually stir in combined wine, water, stock cube, rind and honey. Stir over high heat until mixture boils and thickens.

Strain mixture, whisk in butter; stir in chives. Slice figs, place in hot sauce to heat through. Serve venison sliced with figs and sauce.

Serves 4.

CORIANDER

Also known as Chinese parsley and cilantro, coriander (Coriandrum sativum) is an annual plant, having green fragrant leaves with an insect-like aroma and round bleached-looking seeds that have a warm spicy flavour upon drying. Coriander is native to the Mediterranean region, and is referred to in the Bible and Sanskrit literature. The leaves add a spicy fragrance and exotic flavour to oriental food, and the seeds are used in fish, poultry and meat dishes and in cakes and pastries.

PAN-FRIED FISH WITH SPICY CORIANDER SAUCE

We used barramundi fillets in this recipe but any white fish fillets can be used. Recipe is best made just before serving. This recipe is not suitable to freeze or microwave.

4 medium white fish fillets
plain flour
45g butter
60g butter, extra
¼ teaspoon ground coriander
¼ teaspoon cumin seeds
⅓ cup lime juice
1 tablespoon shredded lime rind
1 tablespoon chopped fresh coriander leaves

Dust fillets lightly with flour, shake away excess flour. Melt butter in medium frying pan, add fillets in single layer, cook over medium heat for about 3 minutes on each side or until tender and golden brown; drain on absorbent paper, keep warm.

Melt extra butter in same pan, add ground coriander and cumin seeds to pan, stir over medium heat for about 1 minute. Stir in juice, rind and fresh coriander, stir over medium heat for 2 minutes. Serve sauce with fillets.

Serves 4.

BELOW: Pan-Fried Fish with Spicy Coriander Sauce.

Below: Plates: Made Where; cutlery: Dansab; cloth: Les Olivades; tiles: Country Floors

CORIANDER GINGER CHICKEN

Chicken can be prepared a day ahead; keep, covered, in refrigerator. Recipe unsuitable to freeze or microwave.

2 cloves garlic, crushed
1 teaspoon grated fresh ginger
¼ cup chopped fresh coriander
¼ cup chopped fresh mint
2 green shallots, finely chopped
¼ cup light soy sauce
¼ cup oil
2 teaspoons castor sugar
8 chicken thigh fillets

Combine garlic, ginger, coriander, mint, shallots, sauce, oil and sugar in large bowl, add chicken; mix well. Cover, refrigerate for several hours or overnight.

Add chicken in single layer to heated greased large frying pan, cook over medium heat for about 5 minutes each side or until tender and golden brown. Brush with remaining marinade during cooking.

Serves 4.

SPICED PUMPKIN AND CORIANDER FLANS

You need to cook 350g pumpkin for this recipe. Flans can be made a day ahead; keep, covered, in refrigerator. This recipe is not suitable to freeze or microwave.

PASTRY

1 cup plain flour
2 teaspoons ground coriander
90g butter
1 egg, lightly beaten

PUMPKIN FILLING

1 tablespoon oil
1 medium onion, chopped
1 clove garlic, crushed
**1 tablespoon chopped fresh
    coriander**
3 eggs, lightly beaten
½ cup thickened cream
½ cup grated Swiss cheese
1 cup mashed pumpkin

Pastry: Sift flour and coriander into medium bowl, rub in butter. Add enough egg to mix to a firm dough. Knead gently on lightly floured surface until smooth, cover, refrigerate for 30 minutes. Roll pastry large enough to line 6 x 10cm deep flan tins. Lift pastry into tins, gently ease pastry into sides of tins, trim edges. Place tins on oven tray, cover pastry with greaseproof paper, fill with dried beans or rice. Bake in moderately hot oven for 10 minutes, remove paper and beans, bake further 7 minutes or until golden brown. Cool pastry shells to room temperature.

Spoon pumpkin filling into pastry shells, bake in moderately hot oven for about 15 minutes or until filling is set and golden brown.

Pumpkin Filling: Heat oil in medium frying pan, add onion, garlic and coriander, stir over medium heat for about 2 minutes (or microwave on HIGH for about 3 minutes) or until onion is soft; cool. Combine remaining ingredients in medium bowl, stir in cooled onion mixture.

Makes 6.

CHICKEN COUSCOUS WITH SPICY TOMATO SAUCE

Chicken can be prepared a day ahead; keep, covered, in refrigerator. Cook just before serving. Recipe unsuitable to freeze or microwave.

¼ cup boiling water
**1 small chicken stock cube,
    crumbled**
¼ cup couscous
15g butter, melted
½ small zucchini, grated
½ small carrot, grated
**1 tablespoon chopped fresh
    coriander**
6 thick chicken breast fillets

*RIGHT: Chicken Couscous with Spicy
Tomato Sauce. LEFT: Spiced Pumpkin and
Coriander Flans. ABOVE LEFT: Coriander
Ginger Chicken.*

plain flour
30g butter
1 tablespoon oil
1 medium onion, chopped
425g can tomato purée
½ teaspoon ground cumin
½ teaspoon ground coriander
¼ teaspoon chilli powder
½ cup dry white wine
½ cup water, extra
**2 tablespoons chopped fresh
    coriander, extra**

Combine boiling water, stock cube and couscous in medium bowl, stand for 10 minutes or until all the water has been absorbed. Stir in butter, zucchini, carrot and fresh coriander.

Using sharp knife, cut a pocket in thickest side of fillets. Spoon couscous mixture into each pocket, secure with toothpicks. Toss fillets in flour, shake away excess flour. Heat butter and oil in medium frying pan, add fillets in single layer, cook over medium heat for about 3 minutes on each side or until golden brown; drain on absorbent paper.

Add onion to pan, stir over medium heat for about 2 minutes or until onion is soft. Stir in purée, cumin, ground coriander, chilli powder, wine and extra water. Bring to boil, reduce heat, simmer, uncovered, for 5 minutes. Return fillets to pan, simmer, uncovered, further 10 minutes or until tender. Stir in extra fresh coriander. Remove toothpicks before serving.

Serves 6.

CHICKEN CORIANDER SOUP

Soup can be made 2 days ahead; keep, covered, in refrigerator, or freeze for up to a month.

4 chicken breast fillets
2 teaspoons oil
2 teaspoons curry powder
1 clove garlic, crushed
1 tablespoon chopped fresh coriander
2 teaspoons chopped fresh basil
1 green shallot, chopped
1 medium tomato, peeled, chopped
2 cups water
1 small chicken stock cube, crumbled
400ml can coconut cream

Cut chicken into thin strips. Heat oil in large saucepan, add curry powder, garlic, coriander, basil and shallot, stir over medium heat for about 1 minute (or microwave on HIGH for about 1 minute) or until shallot is soft.

Add chicken, stir over medium heat for about 4 minutes (or microwave on HIGH for about 3 minutes) or until chicken is almost cooked. Stir in tomato, water and stock cube, bring to boil, reduce heat, cover, simmer for 10 minutes (or microwave on HIGH for 7 minutes). Stir in coconut cream, reheat mixture without boiling.

Serves 4.

SUGAR SNAP PEA AND CORIANDER SOUP

Soup can be made 2 days ahead; keep, covered, in refrigerator. Recipe unsuitable to freeze.

15g butter
3 green shallots, chopped
350g sugar snap peas
1 medium potato, chopped
1 litre (4 cups) water
1½ large chicken stock cubes, crumbled
1 tablespoon chopped fresh coriander
2 tablespoons sour light cream

Melt butter in medium saucepan, add shallots, stir over medium heat for about 2 minutes (or microwave on HIGH for about 2 minutes) or until shallots are soft. Add peas, potato, water and stock cubes to pan, bring to boil, reduce heat, cover, simmer for about 10 minutes (or microwave on HIGH for about 8 minutes) or until peas are just soft.

Blend or process mixture in several batches until smooth. Return mixture to saucepan, bring to boil, remove from heat, stir in coriander and cream.

Serves 6.

MARINATED LAMB WITH CURRY SAUCE

Ask your butcher to bone the loins of lamb for you. Recipe is best made just before serving. Recipe unsuitable to freeze or microwave.

2 x 1½kg loins of lamb, boned
3 small fresh red chillies, chopped
¼ cup chopped fresh coriander leaves
2 teaspoons chopped fresh coriander roots
½ cup olive oil
60g butter
CURRY SAUCE
2 tablespoons oil
1 teaspoon ground coriander
1 teaspoon ground cumin
2 cloves garlic, crushed
2 green shallots, chopped
2 small fresh red chillies, chopped
½ teaspoon ground nutmeg
1 teaspoon ground turmeric
1 tablespoon finely chopped fresh ginger
2 tablespoons tomato paste
400ml can coconut milk
1 cup water
1 large chicken stock cube, crumbled
2 teaspoons brown sugar
1 cinnamon stick

Remove excess fat from loins, cut each loin lengthways into 3 strips. Combine lamb, chillies, coriander leaves, roots and oil in medium bowl, cover, refrigerate overnight.

Melt butter in large frying pan, add lamb in single layer, cook over high heat, turning occasionally, for about 4 minutes or until browned and tender. Cut lamb diagonally into slices. Serve with hot curry sauce and fried noodles, if desired.

Curry Sauce: Heat oil in medium saucepan, add coriander, cumin, garlic, shallots, chillies, nutmeg, turmeric and ginger, stir over medium heat for about 2 minutes. Stir in paste, coconut milk, water, stock cube and sugar, add cinnamon stick. Bring to boil, reduce heat, simmer, uncovered, for about 1 hour, stirring occasionally, until thickened slightly; strain.

Serves 4.

*LEFT: Chicken Coriander Soup.
BELOW LEFT: Sugar Snap Pea and Coriander Soup. BELOW: Marinated Lamb with Curry Sauce.*

Below: Plate: Made Where; chest: Strange Cargo Antiques; fabric: Boyac. Above left: Basket: The Country Trader; fabric: Boyac. Below left: Fabric: Boyac; bucket: The Country Trader

DILL

Both the deep green, ferny leaves and the flat, anise-flavoured seeds are used in cooking. A native to Mediterranean countries, dill (Anethum graveolens) was considered a charm against witchcraft in the Middle Ages. Because of their softness, fresh dill leaves appear to droop and should be kept in the refrigerator in a bowl of water or wrapped in foil. Use to garnish soups and salads, in cooked seafood, herb butter and vinegar. Seeds are used in chutneys, vinegar and dill pickles.

LAMB IN PROSCIUTTO WITH MUSTARD DILL SAUCE

Lamb can be prepared a day ahead; keep, covered, in refrigerator. Cook lamb just before serving. Sauce can be made a day ahead; keep, covered, in refrigerator. This recipe is unsuitable to freeze or microwave.

2 tablespoons oil
30g butter
8 lamb fillets, trimmed
16 slices prosciutto
MUSTARD DILL SAUCE
30g butter
1 clove garlic, crushed
¼ cup dry white wine
3 tablespoons French mustard
¾ cup thickened cream
1 tablespoon chopped fresh dill

Heat oil and butter in large frying pan, add fillets in single layer, cook over high heat until lamb is lightly browned on both sides. Drain on absorbent paper; cool slightly. Wrap each fillet in 2 slices of prosciutto, secure with toothpicks. Add fillets to pan in single layer, cook over high heat, turning frequently, until prosciutto is browned and crisp and lamb is tender. Drain on absorbent paper. Slice fillets before serving with hot sauce.

Mustard Dill Sauce: Melt butter in small saucepan, add garlic, stir over medium heat for 30 seconds, stir in wine, bring to boil, boil, uncovered, until reduced by half. Stir in mustard and cream, stir over medium heat until sauce boils; stir in dill.

Serves 4.

ABOVE: Lamb in Prosciutto with Mustard Dill Sauce.

Above: Plate: The Australian East India Co

LOBSTER AND DILL SOUP

You will need 4 cups of fish stock. Soup can be made 2 days ahead; keep, covered, in refrigerator. Recipe unsuitable to freeze.

250g uncooked lobster tail
30g butter
1 medium onion, chopped
1 clove garlic, crushed
1½ tablespoons plain flour
½ cup dry white wine
2 medium potatoes
½ cup cream
2 tablespoons chopped fresh dill
FISH STOCK
500g fish heads
1½ litres (6 cups) water
1 medium onion, chopped
1 stick celery, chopped
6 black peppercorns, crushed
few parsley stalks

Remove flesh from lobster tail, chop flesh roughly, reserve. Crush lobster shell roughly.

Melt butter in medium saucepan, add onion, garlic and shell. Stir over medium heat for about 2 minutes (or microwave on HIGH for about 3 minutes) or until onion is soft. Stir in flour, stir over medium heat for 1 minute (or microwave on HIGH for 1 minute). Remove from heat, gradually stir in 4 cups of the fish stock and wine, stir over high heat (or microwave on HIGH for about 5 minutes) until mixture boils and thickens; strain.

Cut potatoes into 1cm cubes. Return soup to saucepan, add potatoes and reserved lobster flesh, bring to boil, reduce heat, cover, simmer for about 20 minutes (or microwave on HIGH for about 12 minutes), stirring occasionally, or until potatoes are soft. Blend or process mixture in several batches until smooth, stir in cream and dill. Reheat mixture without boiling.

Fish Stock: Place fish heads, water, onion, celery, peppercorns and parsley in large saucepan. Bring to boil, reduce heat, simmer, uncovered for 20 minutes; strain.

Serves 4.

ABOVE: Lobster and Dill Soup.

43

SPINACH FILLO SPIRALS

Spirals can be prepared 2 days ahead; keep, covered, in refrigerator. Bake just before serving. Recipe can be frozen for 2 months. Spirals are unsuitable to microwave.

250g packet frozen spinach, thawed
¼ cup stale breadcrumbs
2 bacon rashers, chopped
1 medium onion, chopped
½ cup stale breadcrumbs, extra
½ cup grated fresh parmesan cheese
½ cup chopped fresh dill
8 sheets fillo pastry
30g butter, melted
2 tablespoons oil

Add spinach to small frying pan, stir over medium heat for 2 minutes (or microwave on HIGH for 2 minutes). Drain spinach, squeeze out excess moisture. Combine spinach and breadcrumbs in small bowl; mix well.

Add bacon and onion to small frying pan, stir over medium heat for about 3 minutes (or microwave on HIGH for about 2 minutes) or until onion is soft; drain on absorbent paper.

Combine bacon mixture with half the extra breadcrumbs in small bowl; mix well. Combine cheese, dill and remaining extra breadcrumbs in small bowl; mix well.

Layer 4 sheets of pastry, brushing each with combined butter and oil. Spread half the spinach mixture crossways over one-third of the pastry. Spread half the bacon mixture crossways over next one-third of pastry. Sprinkle remaining pastry with half the cheese mixture, leaving 4cm border at the end.

Roll up pastry tightly from the spinach end, place on tray, cover, refrigerate (pictured top right). Repeat process with remaining ingredients.

Cut rolls into 1cm slices (pictured right). Place slices onto greased oven trays and bake in moderately hot oven for about 15 minutes or until golden brown.

Makes about 40.

ABOVE RIGHT: Spinach Fillo Spirals.

Top right: Box: Whitehouse; basket: The Country Trader; whisk and bottle: The Bay Tree

SMOKED COD ROE BALLS WITH DILL TARTARE

Savouries can be made a day ahead; keep, covered, in refrigerator. Tartare sauce can be made 3 days ahead; keep, covered, in refrigerator. Recipe unsuitable to freeze or microwave.

200g smoked cod roe
4 green shallots, chopped
1 cup mashed potato
1¼ cups stale breadcrumbs
¼ cup lemon juice
1 clove garlic, crushed
2 tablespoons chopped fresh dill
1 egg
plain flour
oil for deep-frying
DILL TARTARE
3 egg yolks
1 teaspoon white vinegar
1 cup oil
1 tablespoon lemon juice
1 tablespoon water
2 green shallots, chopped
2 teaspoons drained capers
2 tablespoons chopped fresh dill

Skin the roe, chop roe coarsely. Blend or process roe, shallots, potato, breadcrumbs, juice, garlic, dill and egg until smooth. Transfer mixture to medium bowl, cover, refrigerate mixture for 3 hours.

Shape mixture into small balls, using floured hands. Deep-fry balls in hot oil until browned, drain on absorbent paper. Serve hot with dill tartare.

Dill Tartare: Blend or process yolks and vinegar until pale. Add oil gradually in a thin stream while motor is operating, blend until thick. Stir in juice, water, shallots, capers and dill.

Makes about 40.

SCALLOP AND DILL CONSOMME

Consommé is best made just before serving. Stock can be made a day ahead; keep, covered, in refrigerator or freeze for 3 months.

2 garfish
1½ litres (6 cups) water
1 medium carrot, chopped
1 medium onion, chopped
6 black peppercorns
1 cup water, extra
400g scallops
1 medium leek, thinly sliced
1 teaspoon light soy sauce
125g snow peas
2 teaspoons chopped fresh dill

Remove heads from fish, discard heads. Clean fish, place fish in large saucepan with water, carrot, onion and peppercorns. Bring to boil, reduce heat, cover, simmer for 45 minutes (or microwave on HIGH for 25 minutes). Strain stock, discard fish and vegetables. Place stock into clean large saucepan, add extra water, bring to boil, add scallops, leek and sauce, simmer, uncovered, for 3 minutes (or microwave on HIGH for 2 minutes).

Stir in snow peas and dill, simmer for about 2 minutes (or microwave on HIGH for about 4 minutes) or until the scallops are tender.

Serves 4.

RIGHT: Scallop and Dill Consommé.
ABOVE RIGHT: Smoked Cod Roe Balls with Dill Tartare.

Above right: Plate and bowl: Hampshire & Lowndes; wooden bowl and table: The Country Trader; cloth: Les Olivades

FENNEL

The greenish-yellowy brown seeds, bulbous root stem and feathery, finely-divided green leaves are all used in cooking, most notably with the smaller variety (Florence fennel). Fennel (Foeniculum vulgare) has a sweet, licorice flavour and slightly bitter aftertaste. In 490 BC the Greeks gained a glorious victory over the Persians on the battlefield of Marathon. They gave this name to fennel, which they regarded as a symbol of success. Seeds are used in breads and cakes, the leaves are traditionally used with fish and the bulbs can be added to salads or cooked as a vegetable.

FENNEL BAVAROIS WITH LEMON FENNEL DRESSING

Recipe can be made a day ahead; keep, covered, in refrigerator. Recipe unsuitable to freeze.

30g butter
1 small fennel bulb, chopped
1 small onion, chopped
1 bacon rasher, chopped
125g ricotta cheese
1 tablespoon lemon juice
¾ cup milk
½ cup thickened cream
1 egg, lightly beaten
1 tablespoon chopped fresh
    fennel leaves
3 teaspoons gelatine
1 tablespoon water

LEMON FENNEL DRESSING
2 tablespoons lemon juice
⅓ cup oil
1 tablespoon chopped fresh
    fennel leaves

Melt butter in medium saucepan, add fennel bulb, onion and bacon, stir over medium heat for about 6 minutes (or microwave on HIGH for about 6 minutes) or until fennel is soft.

Blend or process half the fennel mixture with cheese and juice until smooth and creamy.

Combine milk and cream in medium saucepan, bring to boil, whisk in egg, stir over medium heat, without boiling, until mixture thickens slightly.

Combine cheese mixture, milk mixture and fennel leaves with remaining fennel mixture in medium bowl, mix well.

Sprinkle gelatine over water in small bowl, stand in small pan of simmering water, stir until dissolved (or microwave on HIGH for about 20 seconds). Stir into fennel mixture. Pour fennel mixture into 6 oiled moulds (½ cup capacity), cover; refrigerate until set. Turn bavarois onto plates, serve with lemon fennel dressing.
Lemon Fennel Dressing: Combine all ingredients in jar; shake well
    Makes 6.

FENNEL FRITTERS

Recipe is best made close to serving time. This recipe is not suitable to freeze or microwave.

1 tablespoon chopped fresh
    fennel leaves
1 medium fennel bulb, chopped
3 green shallots, chopped
1 small carrot, grated
2 bacon rashers, chopped
2 eggs, lightly beaten
75g ricotta cheese
¼ cup plain flour
2 teaspoons baking powder
oil for shallow-frying

Combine fennel leaves and bulb, shallots, carrot, bacon, eggs, cheese, flour and baking powder in medium bowl; mix well. Shallow-fry heaped tablespoons of mixture in hot oil until golden brown and cooked through; flatten slightly during cooking. Drain on absorbent paper.
    Makes about 16.

LEFT: Fennel Fritters. RIGHT: Fennel Bavarois with Lemon Fennel Dressing.

Left: Plate: Shop 3, Balmain. Right: Plate: Shop 3, Balmain; wooden screen: Mr Brassman

8 whole black peppercorns
1 bay leaf
1½ teaspoons yellow mustard seeds
4 medium fennel bulbs
1½ tablespoons chopped fresh
 fennel leaves

Combine water, oil, vinegar, wine, onion, garlic, peppercorns, bay leaf and mustard seeds in large saucepan. Bring to boil, reduce heat, simmer, uncovered, for 4 minutes (or microwave on HIGH for 5 minutes).

Trim tops from fennel bulbs, cut bulbs in half through centre. Add fennel halves to vinegar mixture in saucepan, bring to boil, reduce heat, simmer, covered, for about 15 minutes (or microwave on HIGH for about 10 minutes) or until just tender. Transfer mixture to large bowl, cool; stir in fennel leaves.

Serves 4 as an entrée.

FENNEL WITH BLUE CHEESE DIP

Recipe is best made just before serving. Recipe is unsuitable to freeze.

2 large fennel bulbs, halved
1 tablespoon chopped fresh
 fennel leaves
CHEESE DIP
30g butter
2 green shallots, chopped
¾ cup milk
75g Stilton cheese, crumbled
75g fontina cheese, finely chopped
75g ricotta cheese

Bring large saucepan of water to the boil, add fennel bulbs, boil, uncovered, for about 15 minutes (or microwave on HIGH for about 10 minutes) or until fennel is just soft. Pull bulbs apart, serve with hot dip sprinkled with fennel leaves.

Cheese Dip: Melt butter in medium saucepan, add shallots, stir over medium heat for 1 minute (or microwave on HIGH for about 1 minute) or until shallots are soft. Stir in milk and cheeses. Whisk over low heat (or microwave on HIGH for about 2 minutes) until cheeses are melted.

Serves 4.

FENNEL AND PRAWNS WITH TOMATO SAUCE

Prepare recipe close to serving time. Recipe unsuitable to freeze.

2 tablespoons oil
2 cloves garlic, crushed
1 medium onion, sliced
1 medium fennel bulb, sliced
410g can tomatoes
½ cup dry white wine
2 tablespoons tomato paste
1kg uncooked medium prawns,
 shelled
2 tablespoons chopped fresh
 fennel leaves
200g feta cheese, crumbled
1 cup black olives

Heat oil in medium saucepan, add garlic, stir over medium heat for 1 minute (or microwave on HIGH for 1 minute). Stir in onion and fennel bulb, stir over medium heat for about 3 minutes (or microwave on HIGH for about 3 minutes) or until onion is soft.

Stir in undrained crushed tomatoes, wine and paste, bring to boil, stir in prawns, simmer, uncovered, for about 5 minutes (or microwave on MEDIUM for about 10 minutes) or until prawns are tender. Stir in fennel leaves and cheese, stir over low heat further minute (or microwave on HIGH for 1 minute), stir in olives. Serve with pasta.

Serves 4.

FENNEL VINAIGRETTE

Recipe can be prepared 3 days ahead; keep, covered, in refrigerator. Recipe unsuitable to freeze.

1½ cups water
¾ cup oil
¾ cup white vinegar
¼ cup dry white wine
1 medium onion, sliced
1 clove garlic, crushed

GARLIC

One of the most famous and popular herbs, garlic (Allium sativum) was most likely used in China, India and Egypt before recorded history. Bulbs of garlic were found in the tomb of Tutankhamon, dating from 1300 BC. Raw garlic juice was used as a field dressing in World War I because of its antiseptic qualities. The peeled, chopped and minced bulbs (made up of segments called cloves) complement nearly all savoury foods, especially the cuisines of Asia and the Mediterranean.

GARLIC AND ONION RELISH

Relish can be made 4 weeks ahead; keep, covered, in refrigerator. Recipe unsuitable to freeze or microwave.

8 medium (1kg) brown onions, chopped
10 cloves garlic, chopped
½ cup oil
½ teaspoon ground allspice
2 teaspoons lime or lemon juice

Combine onions, garlic, oil and allspice in medium saucepan; stir over medium heat until onions are lightly browned. Cover pan, reduce heat, cook over low heat for 1 hour, stirring occasionally. Add juice, blend or process until smooth. Pour into hot sterilised jars, seal when cold. Refrigerate relish until required.

Makes about 1½ cups.

GARLIC, TOMATO AND CHICK PEA STEW

Recipe can be made 3 days ahead; keep, covered, in refrigerator. Recipe unsuitable to freeze or microwave.

1 cup dried chick peas
2 tablespoons olive oil
1 large red Spanish onion, sliced
3 cloves garlic, crushed
3 bacon rashers, chopped
1 medium green pepper, chopped
½ teaspoon paprika
½ teaspoon chilli powder
425g can tomatoes
2 tablespoons tomato paste
½ large vegetable stock cube, crumbled
2 cups water
2 teaspoons chopped fresh oregano

Place chick peas in large bowl, cover with boiling water, cover, stand overnight, drain.

Cook chick peas in large saucepan of boiling water for about 1½ hours or until tender; drain.

Heat oil in large saucepan, add onion, garlic, bacon and pepper, stir over medium heat for about 5 minutes or until onions are soft. Stir in paprika and chilli powder, then undrained crushed tomatoes, paste, stock cube, water and chick peas. Bring to boil, reduce heat, simmer, partly covered, for about 1 hour or until mixture is well thickened. Stir in oregano just before serving.

Serves 4.

BELOW: Garlic, Tomato and Chick Pea Stew. LEFT: Garlic and Onion Relish.

Below: Table and pot: The Country Trader

GARLIC CROUSTADE BASKETS WITH SPINACH SALAD

Croustade baskets can be made several hours ahead; keep in airtight container. Make salad and dressing close to serving time. Recipe unsuitable to freeze or microwave.

1 loaf unsliced white bread
oil for deep-frying
3 cloves garlic, chopped
SPINACH SALAD
1 bunch (40 leaves) English spinach
1 cup bean sprouts
1 small red pepper, thinly sliced
DRESSING
30g butter
⅔ cup French dressing
1 teaspoon French mustard
1 egg
6 anchovy fillets, drained, chopped

Remove crusts from bread, cut bread into 6 thick slices. Hollow out centre from each slice, leaving bases intact to form square basket shapes. Heat enough oil for deep-frying in large saucepan, add garlic, cook baskets 2 at a time in hot oil until golden brown, drain on absorbent paper. Fill baskets with salad, top with dressing.

Spinach Salad: Tear spinach into bite-sized pieces. Combine spinach, sprouts and pepper in medium bowl, toss gently.

Dressing: Melt butter in small saucepan, add dressing and mustard, bring to boil, remove from heat, transfer to small jug. Blend or process egg until smooth, add dressing mixture gradually in a thin stream while motor is operating, blend until smooth. Transfer mixture to bowl, stir in anchovies just before using.

Serves 6.

ABOVE: Marinated Tuna with Garlic Vinaigrette. LEFT: Garlic Croustade Baskets with Spinach Salad.

Above: Plate and cups: Made in Japan. Left: Plate: Studio-Haus

MARINATED TUNA WITH GARLIC VINAIGRETTE

Prepare close to serving time. Recipe unsuitable to freeze or microwave.

500g fresh tuna
¼ teaspoon freshly ground salt
¼ cup olive oil
2 tablespoons white wine vinegar
1 tablespoon lemon juice
2 cloves garlic, crushed
1 small fresh red chilli, chopped
1 teaspoon sugar
1 small green cucumber

Cut tuna into thin slices, place in single layer on plastic tray or plastic-wrap-covered Swiss roll pan; sprinkle tuna with salt. Pour combined oil, vinegar, juice, garlic, chilli and sugar over tuna, cover, refrigerate for 1 hour.

Slice cucumber into ribbons using vegetable peeler. To serve, place slices of tuna and cucumber onto plate, top with a little of the dressing.

Serves 6.

PRAWNS KIEV

Recipe can be prepared a day ahead; keep, covered, in refrigerator. Recipe unsuitable to freeze or microwave.

90g butter
1 tablespoon chopped fresh
flat-leafed parsley
2 teaspoons seeded mustard
4 cloves garlic, crushed
20 uncooked king prawns
plain flour
2 eggs, lightly beaten
⅓ cup milk
packaged breadcrumbs
oil for deep-frying

Combine butter, parsley, mustard and garlic in small bowl (or process all ingredients until smooth). Place butter mixture onto foil, shape into 30cm roll, wrap in foil, refrigerate until firm. Cut butter into 10 x 3cm slices.

Shell and devein prawns. Gently pound 2 prawns together into a flat circle, repeat with remaining prawns.

With wet hands, mould each prawn circle around each butter slice.

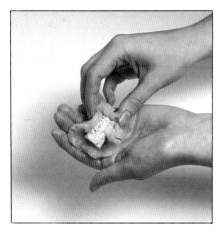

Toss prawns in flour, shake away excess flour, dip into combined eggs and milk, then in breadcrumbs. Dip in egg mixture again, then breadcrumbs; refrigerate. Deep-fry in hot oil until cooked through and golden brown.

Makes 10.

RIGHT: Prawns Kiev.

GARLIC PIZZETTA WITH SMOKED SALMON

Pizzetta is best prepared close to serving time. Crème fraîche must be prepared 2 days ahead. Recipe unsuitable to freeze or microwave.

¼ teaspoon sugar
7g sachet dried yeast
¼ cup plain flour
½ cup warm water
1 tablespoon milk
3 cloves garlic, crushed
1¾ cups plain flour, extra
1 teaspoon salt
2 tablespoons olive oil
2 tablespoons tomato paste
1 medium onion, thinly sliced
2 tablespoons capers, drained
4 thin slices smoked salmon, chopped
¼ cup olive oil, extra
2 cloves garlic, crushed, extra
2 tablespoons chopped fresh parsley
1 cup grated fresh parmesan cheese

CREME FRAICHE
¾ cup thickened cream
2 tablespoons buttermilk

Lightly grease 30cm pizza pan. Combine sugar and yeast in small bowl, stir in flour and water, cover, stand in warm place for about 10 minutes or until mixture is foamy. Stir milk and garlic into yeast mixture.

Sift extra flour and salt into large bowl, stir in yeast mixture, then oil. Turn dough onto lightly floured surface, knead for about 10 minutes or until dough is smooth and elastic. Place dough in lightly oiled bowl, cover, stand in warm place for about 45 minutes or until doubled in size.

Knead dough until smooth. Roll dough into circle about 34cm diameter, place into pizza pan, twist and roll edges to fit pan. Spread dough with paste, top with onion, capers and salmon. Combine extra oil, extra garlic and parsley in jug, pour over pizza. Sprinkle cheese around edge of pizza, bake in moderately hot oven for about 25 minutes or until golden brown. Serve with crème fraîche.

Crème Fraîche: Combine cream with buttermilk in small bowl; stand, covered, in warm place for 48 hours or until cream thickens; refrigerate before using.

GARLIC AND HERB MUSSELS

Mussels are best prepared close to serving time. Recipe unsuitable to freeze or microwave.

1kg small mussels
⅓ cup olive oil
6 cloves garlic, crushed
¼ cup chopped fresh parsley
2 tablespoons chopped fresh basil
¼ cup lemon juice

Scrub mussels under cold water, remove beards. Heat oil in large frying pan, add garlic, parsley, basil and juice, cook over medium heat for 5 minutes. Add mussels, bring to boil, boil, covered, for about 2 minutes. Remove mussels as they open and place in serving bowls.

Boil liquid, uncovered, for about 5 minutes or until thickened. Pour over mussels just before serving.

Serves 4.

GRILLED CHICKEN KEBABS WITH GARLIC SAUCE

Soak wooden skewers in water for several hours or overnight to prevent burning during cooking. Chicken can be prepared a day ahead; keep, covered, in refrigerator. Recipe unsuitable to freeze or microwave.

500g chicken thigh fillets
¼ cup lime juice
2 tablespoons oil

GARLIC SAUCE
3 cloves garlic, crushed
½ cup stale breadcrumbs
¼ cup lime juice
¼ cup oil
1 teaspoon castor sugar
2 tablespoons chopped fresh parsley

Cut chicken into 2cm pieces, combine with juice and oil in medium bowl, cover, refrigerate for 1 hour. Thread chicken onto skewers, grill on both sides, basting frequently with marinade, until chicken is tender. Serve with sauce.

Garlic Sauce: Blend or process all ingredients until well combined.

Serves 4.

ABOVE: Garlic Pizzetta with Smoked Salmon. RIGHT: From top: Garlic and Herb Mussels; Grilled Chicken Kebabs with Garlic Sauce.

Above: Table: Country Form. Right: Plates, basket and background screen: Corso de Fiori

GINGER

Ginger (Zingiber officinale) was one of the first Oriental spices to reach Europe from its native Asia, in the ancient spice trade. Ginger's discovery in China was first written about by Marco Polo. The fresh tang and distinctive heat of ginger forms the basis of many Asian dishes. Ginger is also used in preserves, sweets, biscuits, gingerbread, and cakes and has a tenderising effect when used on meat. The thick tuberous rhizome (or root) should be peeled and grated or sliced thinly.

BARBECUED GINGER PORK

Best prepared just before serving. This recipe is not suitable to freeze or microwave.

8 pork butterfly steaks
1 tablespoon brown sugar
1 tablespoon oil
2 tablespoons grated fresh ginger
¼ teaspoon five spice powder
1 tablespoon hoisin sauce
1 tablespoon light soy sauce
¼ cup green ginger wine
1 clove garlic, crushed

Place pork in shallow dish. Combine remaining Ingredients, pour over pork, cover, refrigerate for several hours or overnight. Barbecue or grill pork, basting with marinade, until tender.
Serves 4.

GINGERED SNAPPER CUTLETS

Cutlet parcels can be prepared a day ahead; keep, covered, in refrigerator. Recipe unsuitable to freeze.

4 medium snapper cutlets
60g butter
2 teaspoons chopped fresh chives
2 teaspoons chopped fresh parsley
GINGERED VEGETABLES
1 medium leek
1 medium carrot
2 teaspoons oil
15g butter
1 clove garlic, sliced
2 tablespoons finely chopped
   fresh ginger
2 tablespoons green ginger wine

LEFT: Barbecued Ginger Pork.
RIGHT: Gingered Snapper Cutlets.

Right: Plate, scarf and cutlery: Made Where

Cut 4 circles of baking paper large enough to enclose individual cutlets. Place a cutlet on half of each circle, top with gingered vegetables. Fold paper securely over cutlets, tuck ends under. Place parcels on oven tray, bake in moderate oven for about 20 minutes (or microwave on MEDIUM for about 12 minutes) or until fish is tender. Melt butter in small saucepan, add chives and parsley. Remove fish and vegetables from paper, place on plates, top with butter mixture.

Gingered Vegetables: Cut leek into thin strips about 5cm long. Using vegetable peeler, peel carrot into thin strips lengthways. Heat oil and butter in medium frying pan, add garlic and ginger, stir over medium heat for 1 minute (or microwave on HIGH for about 1 minute). Add leek, carrot and ginger wine. Stir over medium heat for about 1 minute (or microwave on HIGH for about 1 minute) or until vegetables are wilted.

Serves 4.

GINGER PRAWN FLANS

Pastry cases can be made a day ahead; keep in airtight container. Filling is best made just before serving. This recipe is not suitable to freeze or microwave.

PASTRY
1 cup plain flour
90g butter
1 egg yolk
**3 teaspoons lemon juice,
    approximately**
GINGER PRAWN FILLING
30g butter
1 tablespoon oil
1 tablespoon grated fresh ginger
1 clove garlic, crushed
**1 small fresh red chilli, finely
    chopped**
2 tablespoons plain flour
750g uncooked king prawns, shelled
1 tablespoon honey

½ cup dry white wine
½ cup cream
2 tablespoons chopped fresh chives
Pastry: Sift flour into medium bowl, rub in butter. Add egg yolk and enough juice to make ingredients cling together. Knead gently on lightly floured surface until smooth; cover, refrigerate for 30 minutes.

Divide pastry into 6 portions, roll portions large enough to line 6 x 8cm flan tins. Lift pastry into flan tins, gently ease pastry into sides of tins; trim edges. Place tins on oven tray, cover pastry with greaseproof paper, fill with dried beans or rice. Bake in moderately hot oven for 7 minutes.

Remove paper and beans, bake pastry for further 7 minutes or until lightly browned, cool to room temperature. Pour filling into pastry cases, sprinkle filling with toasted shredded coconut, if desired.

Ginger Prawn Filling: Heat butter and oil in large frying pan, add ginger, garlic and chilli, stir over medium heat for 2 minutes, stir in flour, stir over medium heat for 1 minute. Add prawns, honey, wine and cream. Stir over high heat until sauce boils and thickens and prawns are tender; stir in chives.

Makes 6.

FRIED CHICKEN
GINGER CREPES

Recipe is best prepared close to serving time. Unfilled crêpes can be made a day ahead; keep, layered with greaseproof paper, in refrigerator. Crêpes can be frozen for 2 months. You will need half a small barbecued chicken for this recipe. Recipe unsuitable to freeze or microwave.

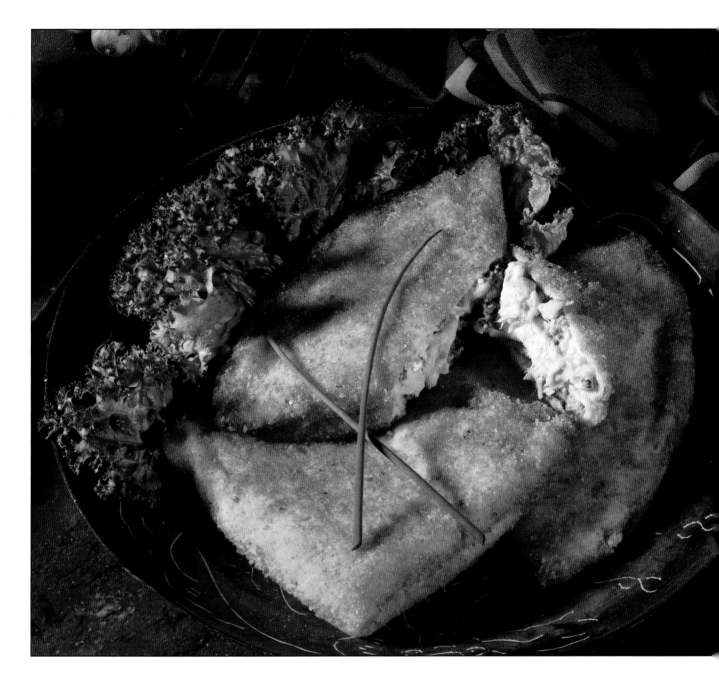

CREPES
½ **cup plain flour**
2 eggs
¾ **cup milk**
2 eggs, lightly beaten, extra
¾ **cup packaged breadcrumbs**
¾ **cup cornflake crumbs**
oil for shallow-frying
CHICKEN GINGER FILLING
100g broccoli, chopped
30g butter
2 green shallots, chopped
2 tablespoons plain flour
½ **small chicken stock cube,
   crumbled**
¾ **cup water**
1 cup chopped cooked chicken
¼ **cup chopped unroasted unsalted
   cashew nuts**
½ **cup alfalfa sprouts**
1 tablespoon grated fresh ginger
¼ **cup sour cream**

Crêpes: Sift flour into medium bowl, make well in centre, gradually stir in combined eggs and milk, mix to a smooth batter (or blend or process all ingredients until smooth). Cover, stand for 30 minutes. Pour 2 to 3 tablespoons of batter into heated greased heavy-based crêpe pan; cook until lightly browned underneath. Turn crêpe, brown on other side. Repeat with remaining batter. You need 8 crêpes for this recipe.

Spread filling over half of each crêpe, fold crêpes into triangles. Dip crêpe in extra eggs, then in combined breadcrumbs and cornflake crumbs. Shallow-fry crêpes in hot oil until golden brown on both sides; drain on absorbent paper.

Chicken Ginger Filling: Boil, steam or microwave broccoli until just tender; drain. Melt butter in medium saucepan, add shallots, stir over medium heat for

about 1 minute (or microwave on HIGH for about 1 minute) or until shallots are soft. Stir in flour, stir over medium heat for 1 minute (or microwave on HIGH for 1 minute).

Remove from heat, gradually stir in combined stock cube and water, stir over high heat (or microwave on HIGH for about 3 minutes) until mixture boils and thickens.

Stir in broccoli and remaining ingredients, reheat without boiling.

Serves 4 as an entrée.

ABOVE: Fried Chicken Ginger Crêpes.
ABOVE LEFT: Ginger Prawn Flans.

Above left: Tiles: Country Floors

61

GINGER SOUFFLES

Recipe is best made just before serving. This recipe is unsuitable to freeze or microwave.

2 tablespoons grated fresh ginger
60g butter
¼ cup castor sugar
2 tablespoons plain flour
1 tablespoon cornflour
2 teaspoons ground ginger
1 cup milk
3 eggs, separated
2 tablespoons chopped glacé ginger
1 egg white, extra

Grease 4 soufflé dishes (1 cup capacity), sprinkle base and sides with a little extra sugar.

Press ginger between 2 spoons to extract 1 tablespoon juice, reserve juice, discard pulp.

Cream butter and sugar in small bowl with electric mixer until light and fluffy, beat in sifted flours and ground ginger. Heat milk in small saucepan, gradually stir in creamed butter mixture; stir over medium heat until mixture boils and thickens. Remove from heat, quickly stir in egg yolks, reserved ginger juice and glacé ginger, transfer mixture to large bowl.

Beat all egg whites in small bowl until soft peaks form, fold into ginger mixture in 2 batches. Pour mixture into prepared dishes. Bake in moderately hot oven for about 15 minutes or until puffed and golden brown.

Serves 4.

GINGER BAVAROIS WITH APRICOT SAUCE

Bavarois and sauce can be made 2 days ahead; keep, covered, in refrigerator. Cointreau is an orange-flavoured liqueur. Recipe unsuitable to freeze or microwave.

3 egg yolks
¼ cup castor sugar
2 cups milk
2 tablespoons grated fresh ginger
1 tablespoon gelatine
2 tablespoons water
1 tablespoon lime juice
½ cup thickened cream
APRICOT SAUCE
425g can apricot halves
1 tablespoon sugar
1 tablespoon Cointreau

Beat egg yolks and sugar in small bowl with electric mixer until thick and creamy. Heat milk in medium saucepan until almost boiling. Gradually whisk milk into egg mixture. Transfer mixture to large bowl.

Press ginger between 2 spoons to extract 1 tablespoon juice; reserve juice, discard pulp.

Sprinkle gelatine over combined

ginger juice, water and lime juice in small bowl, stand in small saucepan of simmering water, stir until dissolved (or microwave on HIGH for about 30 seconds). Whisk gelatine mixture into egg mixture, cool to room temperature. Beat cream until soft peaks form, fold into egg mixture.

Pour mixture into 6 lightly oiled moulds (½ cup capacity); refrigerate until set. Turn onto plates, serve with apricot sauce.

Apricot Sauce: Blend or process undrained apricots, sugar and liqueur until smooth.

Serves 6.

PRAWN AND GINGER PUFFS

Keep unfilled puffs in airtight container for a week or freeze for a month. Re-crisp puffs in moderate oven for a few minutes, fill close to serving time. Puffs are unsuitable to microwave. Sauce is best made just before serving. Sauce is unsuitable to freeze.

CHOUX PASTRY
75g butter, chopped
1 cup water
1 cup plain flour
4 eggs, lightly beaten

PRAWN AND GINGER FILLING
30g butter
2 green shallots, chopped
1 small red pepper, finely sliced
2 tablespoons grated fresh ginger
1 tablespoon dry white wine
2 teaspoons lemon juice
½ teaspoon French mustard
1 teaspoon sugar
1 tablespoon plain flour
¼ cup cream
¾ cup milk
1kg uncooked king prawns, shelled, chopped

Choux Pastry: Combine butter and water in saucepan, bring to boil, stirring, until butter is melted. Add flour all at once. Stir vigorously over medium heat with wooden spoon until mixture leaves side of pan and forms a smooth ball. Place mixture in small bowl of electric mixer (or in processor). Add eggs gradually, beating well on low speed after each addition. Mixture should be glossy.

Spoon mixture into large piping bag fitted with plain tube. Pipe 5cm lengths of pastry, 5cm apart, onto lightly greased oven trays. Bake in hot oven for 10 minutes, reduce heat to moderate, bake further 15 minutes or until well puffed and lightly browned.

Make a small slit in side of each puff to allow steam to escape, return to moderate oven for about 10 minutes or until dry and crisp. Cut puffs in half, remove any doughy centres, spoon in hot filling.

Prawn and Ginger Filling: Heat butter in medium saucepan, add shallots, pepper, ginger and wine, stir over low heat for about 4 minutes (or microwave on HIGH for about 3 minutes) or until pepper is soft.

Add juice, mustard, sugar and flour, stir over high heat for 1 minute (or microwave on HIGH for 1 minute).

Remove from heat, gradually stir in cream and milk, stir over high heat (or microwave on HIGH for about 3 minutes) until mixture boils and thickens. Stir in prawns, stir over high heat for about 2 minutes (or microwave on HIGH for about 2 minutes) or until prawns are tender.

Makes 16.

ABOVE LEFT: Ginger Soufflés.
BELOW LEFT: Ginger Bavarois with Apricot Sauce. BELOW: Prawn and Ginger Puffs.

Below: Plate: Noritake. Below left: Plate: Studio—Haus; napkin: Les Olivades; cupboard: Whitehall

GINGER CUSTARDS WITH CARAMEL SAUCE

Custards are best prepared a day ahead; keep, covered, in refrigerator. Sauce is best prepared close to serving time. Recipe unsuitable to freeze or microwave.

4 eggs
¼ cup castor sugar
1 cup milk
1 cup thickened cream
1 tablespoon grated fresh ginger
CARAMEL SAUCE
½ cup castor sugar
¼ cup water
¾ cup orange juice
2 tablespoons brandy
60g butter

Lightly grease 4 ovenproof dishes (¾ cup capacity). Lightly whisk eggs and sugar together in medium bowl. Combine milk, cream and ginger in small saucepan, bring to boil, remove from heat, allow bubbles to subside. Gradually whisk into egg mixture.

Pour mixture into prepared dishes. Place dishes into baking dish, pour in enough boiling water to come halfway up sides of dishes. Bake in moderate oven for about 30 minutes or until custards are set. Remove dishes from water, cool to room temperature, refrigerate overnight. Turn custards onto plates, serve with caramel sauce and extra whipped cream, if desired.

Caramel Sauce: Combine sugar and water in medium saucepan, stir over high heat, without boiling, until sugar is dissolved. Bring to boil, boil, without stirring, for about 5 minutes or until mixture turns golden brown, remove from heat. Carefully stir in juice (it will bubble fiercely), return to heat, stir over medium heat for about 5 minutes or until caramel is melted. Stir in brandy and butter.

Serves 4.

ABOVE: Ginger Custards with Caramel Sauce.

China: Royal Worcester

HORSERADISH

Horseradish (Cochlearia armoracia), a perennial relative to the mustard family, has large, spinach-like leaves and a pungent white tap root with a sharp, burning flavour and biting aroma. In the 13th century, it was used as a medicine, seasoning and leaf vegetable in its native Europe, and by the 16th century, was known in England. Use the grated or sliced root in sauces, mustards, and in sour cream dressings. Horseradish sauce is traditional with roast and corned beef.

SMOKED EEL PARCELS WITH HORSERADISH BUTTER

Parcels can be prepared 2 days ahead; keep, covered, in refrigerator. Cook parcels just before serving. Butter can be made a week ahead; keep, covered, in refrigerator. Recipe unsuitable to freeze or microwave.

6 smoked eel fillets
6 sheets fillo pastry
60g butter, melted
HORSERADISH BUTTER
45g butter, softened
2 tablespoons mayonnaise
½ teaspoon seeded mustard
¼ cup grated fresh horseradish
2 teaspoons chopped fresh parsley
1 small gherkin, finely chopped

Cut each eel fillet in half crossways. Layer 2 sheets of pastry together, brushing each sheet with butter. Cut pastry in half lengthways. Place a piece of eel on narrow end of each piece of pastry, fold edges of pastry in, roll up. Repeat with remaining pastry, butter and eel. Place parcels on lightly greased oven tray. Bake in moderately hot oven for about 8 minutes or until brown. Serve with horseradish butter.

Horseradish Butter: Beat butter in small bowl with electric mixer until light and fluffy. Stir in mayonnaise, mustard, horseradish, parsley and gherkin. Spoon mixture into piping bag fitted with star tube. Pipe mixture onto greaseproof paper, refrigerate mixture until firm.

Makes 6.

LEFT: Smoked Eel Parcels with Horseradish Butter.

Plate and fork: Studio-Haus

RACKS OF LAMB WITH HORSERADISH SEASONING

This recipe is not suitable to freeze or microwave.

2 racks of lamb (6 cutlets in each)
½ cup chopped fresh parsley
½ cup grated fresh horseradish
2 cups (200g) stale breadcrumbs
30g butter, melted
1 teaspoon grated lemon rind
1 tablespoon lemon juice
HORSERADISH CREAM
1 tablespoon lemon juice
1 clove garlic, crushed
1 egg yolk
1 tablespoon grated fresh horseradish
½ cup olive oil

Trim racks, remove excess fat. Using sharp knife, separate bones from meat, leaving both ends intact to form a pocket. Cover bones with foil.

Combine parsley, horseradish, breadcrumbs, butter, rind and juice in small bowl; mix well. Press mixture firmly into lamb pockets, place onto rack in baking dish, bake in moderate oven for about 40 minutes or until tender and browned. Cut racks into cutlets, serve with horseradish cream.

Horseradish Cream: Blend or process juice, garlic, yolk and horseradish until smooth. With motor operating, add oil gradually in a thin stream, process until mixture is thick.

Serves 4 to 6.

BELOW: Racks of Lamb with Horseradish Seasoning.

Plate: Shop 3, Balmain

FILLET OF BEEF
WITH HORSERADISH CREAM

Beef is best cooked close to serving time. Cream can be made 3 days ahead; keep, covered, in refrigerator. This recipe is unsuitable to freeze or microwave.

2 x 750g pieces beef eye fillet
2 teaspoons cracked black
**   peppercorns**
90g butter
2 tablespoons plain flour
2 small beef stock cubes, crumbled
2 cups water
2 tablespoons brandy
200g baby mushrooms, sliced
HORSERADISH CREAM
½ cup chopped fresh horseradish
2 tablespoons lemon juice
1 tablespoon water
½ cup sour cream
Trim excess fat from beef. Secure with string at 5cm intervals. Press peppercorns firmly onto beef. Melt butter in large baking dish, add beef, cook over high heat for about 5 minutes or until browned all over. Bake in moderately hot oven for about 20 minutes for rare beef or 30 minutes for medium rare beef. Remove beef from dish, remove string, keep warm.

Pour excess drippings from dish, leaving ¼ cup in dish, stir in flour, stir over medium heat for about 5 minutes or until flour is browned. Remove from heat, gradually stir in combined stock cubes, water, brandy and mushrooms, stir over high heat until sauce boils and thickens. Serve sliced beef with sauce and horseradish cream.

Horseradish Cream: Blend or process horseradish, juice and water until smooth; stir in sour cream.

Serves 6.

ABOVE: Fillet of Beef with Horseradish Cream.

Plate and cutlery: Studio-Haus

LEMON BALM

This delicately lemon-scented member of the mint family is a perennial with soft, wrinkled leaves. The sweet aroma of balm (Melissa officinalis) led to its name, an abbreviation of balsam. For centuries, bee hives have been rubbed with balm in order to prevent the bees from swarming, particularly in its native Southern Europe. Balm is used in fruit drinks, fruit salads and many savoury dishes.

ORANGE AND PEPPER SALAD

Dressing can be made 2 days ahead; keep, covered, in refrigerator. Recipe unsuitable to freeze.

2 medium red peppers, sliced
4 medium oranges, segmented
2 green shallots, chopped
LEMON BALM DRESSING
¼ cup oil
1 tablespoon white wine vinegar
1 clove garlic, crushed
1 tablespoon chopped fresh
**   lemon balm**

Combine peppers, oranges and shallots in large bowl; mix well. Pour over dressing; cover, refrigerate for several hours before serving.
Lemon Balm Dressing: Combine all ingredients in jar; shake well.
    Serves 4.

SPICY LIME CHICKEN STIR-FRY

Recipe is best made close to serving time. This recipe is not suitable to freeze or microwave.

4 chicken breast fillets, chopped
plain flour
2 tablespoons oil
30g butter
4 green shallots, chopped
1 medium red pepper, chopped
1 clove garlic, crushed
2 teaspoons grated fresh ginger
2 small fresh green chillies, chopped
1 teaspoon grated lime rind
2 tablespoons lime juice
1 tablespoon sugar
2 tablespoons light soy sauce
2 tablespoons hoisin sauce
1 large chicken stock cube,
**   crumbled**
1 tablespoon cornflour
1 cup water
2 tablespoons chopped fresh
**   lemon balm**

Toss chicken in flour; shake away excess flour. Heat oil and butter in large frying pan or wok. Add chicken, shallots, pepper, garlic, ginger and chillies, stir over medium heat for about 5 minutes or until chicken is tender. Stir in combined rind, juice, sugar, sauces and stock cube. Blend cornflour with water, stir into chicken mixture, stir over high heat until mixture boils and thickens. Stir in lemon balm.
    Serves 4.

LEFT: Orange and Pepper Salad. RIGHT: Spicy Lime Chicken Stir-Fry.

Left: Plate: The Antique General Store. Right: Bowl and wheelbarrow: The Antique General Store

GOOSEBERRY AND LEMON BALM JELLY

We used Granny Smith apples in this recipe. Jelly will keep in a cool place for 2 months. Jelly unsuitable to freeze or microwave.

4 large (800g) apples
1kg fresh or frozen gooseberries
2 tablespoons lemon juice
1 tablespoon chopped fresh
    lemon balm

3 cups water
3 cups sugar, approximately
⅓ cup chopped fresh
    lemon balm, extra

Chop unpeeled apples roughly. Place apples, gooseberries, juice, lemon balm and water in large saucepan, cover, bring to boil, reduce heat, simmer for about 30 minutes or until fruit is very soft. Strain mixture through fine cloth. Allow mixture to drip through cloth slowly, discard pulp.

Measure liquid, pour into large saucepan. Add 1 cup sugar to each 1 cup liquid. Mixture should not be more than 5cm deep at this stage. Stir over high heat, without boiling, until sugar is dissolved. Bring to boil, boil, uncovered, without stirring, for about 15 minutes or until jelly sets when tested on a cold saucer. Stand 5 minutes, stir in extra lemon balm. Pour into hot sterilised jars, seal when cold.

Makes about 3 cups.

SPICY LEMON BALM LENTILS

Recipe is best made close to serving time. Recipe unsuitable to freeze.

1 cup brown lentils
1 tablespoon oil
1 large onion, chopped
2 cloves garlic, crushed
1 teaspoon grated fresh ginger
2 small fresh red chillies, chopped
1 teaspoon ground coriander
1 teaspoon ground turmeric
½ teaspoon lemon pepper seasoning
425g can tomatoes
1 tablespoon tomato paste
2 tablespoons lemon juice
¼ cup chopped fresh lemon balm

Soak lentils in large bowl of water overnight. Drain lentils, add to medium saucepan of boiling water, boil, uncovered, for about 20 minutes or until lentils are tender; drain.

Heat oil in medium saucepan, add onion, stir over medium heat for about 3 minutes (or microwave on HIGH for about 4 minutes) or until onion is soft. Stir in garlic, ginger, chillies, coriander, turmeric and lemon pepper, stir over medium heat for further minute (or microwave on HIGH for 1 minute).

Stir in undrained crushed tomatoes and paste, bring to boil, reduce heat, cover, simmer for 10 minutes, stirring occasionally (or microwave on HIGH for 5 minutes). Stir in lentils, juice and lemon balm, stir over medium heat (or microwave on HIGH for about 2 minutes) until mixture is hot.

Serves 4.

ICED LEMON BALM TEA

Tea can be made a day ahead; keep, covered, in refrigerator.

1 litre (4 cups) boiling water
⅔ cup chopped fresh lemon balm

Pour water over lemon balm in large bowl, cool, refrigerate several hours. Strain before serving.

Makes 1 litre (4 cups).

LEFT: Gooseberry and Lemon Balm Jelly.
RIGHT: Iced Lemon Balm Tea.
ABOVE RIGHT: Spicy Lemon Balm Lentils.

Left: Table: Country Form. Right: Cup and saucer: Casa Shopping. Above right: Coffee pot, treasure chest and rug: Mr Brass Man

LEMON GRASS

Known in Asia as serai or sereh, and in Thailand as takrai, lemon grass (Cymbopogan citratus) has long, thin leaves with a rough, sticky texture and a delicious lemon scent. It was virtually unknown to the western world until recent times, when Asian immigrants introduced it from its native habitat to Europeans, Americans and Australians. The lower, more tender part of the leaf should be used in cooking, and is used frequently in Thai and Malaysian recipes, curries, baked fish and chicken.

LIME PICKLE WITH LEMON GRASS

This is an Indian-style pickle; serve with curries. Pickle can be stored in refrigerator for 2 months. Recipe unsuitable to freeze or microwave.

10 medium limes, sliced
2 teaspoons coarse cooking salt
1 cup oil
4 small fresh green chillies, chopped
2 teaspoons chilli powder
1 tablespoon grated fresh ginger
6 cloves garlic, crushed
1 tablespoon chopped fresh
  lemon grass
1 teaspoon yellow mustard seeds
2 cups white wine vinegar

Combine limes and salt in large glass bowl; cover, stand overnight. Rinse limes under cold water; drain. Heat oil in large saucepan, add chillies, chilli powder, ginger, garlic, lemon grass and mustard seeds, stir over medium heat for 2 minutes. Stir in limes and vinegar, stir over medium heat for 10 minutes. Pour pickle into hot sterilised jars; seal when cold. Store for a week before using.
  Makes about 1¼ litres (5 cups).

LAMB CURRY WITH COCONUT CREAM

Curry is best made a day ahead; keep, covered, in refrigerator, or freeze for 2 months. This recipe is not suitable to microwave.

1kg lamb fillets, chopped
2 tablespoons drained canned green
  peppercorns, crushed
plain flour
2 tablespoons oil
60g butter
2 green shallots, chopped
2 cloves garlic, crushed
2 tablespoons chopped fresh
  lemon grass
2 teaspoons chopped fresh
  coriander
1 teaspoon grated fresh ginger
¼ teaspoon ground coriander
¼ teaspoon ground cumin
¼ teaspoon ground nutmeg
1 teaspoon grated lemon rind
2 small fresh green chillies, chopped
400ml can coconut cream
2 teaspoons sugar
1 teaspoon fish sauce
⅔ cup roasted unsalted peanuts,
  chopped

Combine lamb and peppercorns in large bowl, stand for 30 minutes. Toss lamb in flour, shake away excess flour. Heat oil in large saucepan, add lamb in batches, stir over high heat until lamb is well browned all over; drain on absorbent paper. Discard oil in pan.
  Melt butter in same pan, add shallots, garlic, lemon grass, coriander, ginger, spices, rind and chillies, stir over medium heat for about 3 minutes or until shallots and chillies are soft. Blend or process mixture until smooth.
  Return lamb to pan, stir in spice mixture, cook, covered, over low heat for about 45 minutes or until lamb is tender. Stir in remaining ingredients. Reheat mixture without boiling.
  Serves 6.

LEFT: Lime Pickle with Lemon Grass.
RIGHT: Lamb Curry with Coconut Cream.

Left: Bowl and fabric: Gallery Nomad. Right: Basket and casserole dish: Australian East India Co.

CHICKEN AND LEMON GRASS STIR-FRY

Recipe is best made just before serving. This recipe is not suitable to freeze or microwave.

2 tablespoons oil
1 teaspoon sesame oil
¼ cup chopped fresh lemon grass
1 clove garlic, crushed
1 small fresh red chilli, chopped
4 chicken breast fillets, chopped
2 teaspoons cornflour
¼ cup water
1 tablespoon fish sauce
1 tablespoon oyster sauce
½ teaspoon sugar
½ x 230g can water chestnuts, chopped
1 medium green pepper, sliced

Heat oils in wok or large frying pan, add lemon grass, garlic and chilli, stir-fry for 1 minute. Add chicken, stir-fry in 2 batches for about 4 minutes or until tender. Blend cornflour with water, stir into chicken mixture with sauces and sugar. Stir over high heat until mixture boils and thickens. Stir in chestnuts and pepper, stir over medium heat further minute.

Serves 4.

PRAWN STIR-FRY WITH LEMON GRASS AND TAMARIND

Stir-fry is best prepared close to serving time. Recipe unsuitable to freeze or microwave.

1kg uncooked king prawns, shelled
2 tablespoons oil
1 clove garlic, crushed
2 teaspoons grated fresh ginger
2 tablespoons chopped fresh lemon grass
4 green shallots, chopped
1 medium red pepper, sliced
2 tablespoons tamarind sauce
½ cup water
1 small chicken stock cube, crumbled
2 teaspoons cornflour
1 tablespoon water, extra

Cut almost through backs of prawns, remove dark veins. Press prawns open gently along cut side with knife.

Heat oil in wok or large frying pan, add garlic, ginger, lemon grass and shallots, stir-fry over high heat for about 2 minutes or until shallots are soft. Add pepper and prawns, stir-fry over high heat for about 2 minutes or until prawns are just cooked.

Stir in combined sauce, water and stock cube, stir-fry over high heat for 1 minute. Blend cornflour with extra water, stir into wok, stir-fry over high heat until sauce boils and thickens.

Serves 4.

ABOVE: Chicken and Lemon Grass Stir-Fry. RIGHT: Prawn Stir-Fry with Lemon Grass and Tamarind. ABOVE RIGHT: Beef Satays with Lemon Grass Marinade.

Above: Bowls, tray and mats: Australian East India Co. Right: Background: House of Bambuzit. Above right: Platter and fabric: Corso de Fiori; pewter plate: The Country Trader

BEEF SATAYS WITH LEMON GRASS MARINADE

Steak can be marinated a day ahead; keep, covered, in refrigerator. If using bamboo skewers, soak in water for at least 1 hour before using. Recipe unsuitable to freeze or microwave.

200ml carton coconut cream
1 tablespoon crunchy peanut butter
2 teaspoons sambal oelek
2 tablespoons chopped fresh
   lemon grass
2 cloves garlic, crushed
1 teaspoon ground coriander
1 teaspoon ground turmeric
750g rump steak

Combine coconut cream, peanut butter, sambal oelek, lemon grass, garlic, coriander and turmeric in large bowl. Cut steak into 2cm cubes, add to marinade; mix well. Cover, refrigerate for several hours or overnight.

Remove meat from marinade, thread onto skewers. Grill or barbecue satays until meat is tender; brush with remaining marinade during cooking.

Makes 12.

MARJORAM

This close relative to oregano has small grey-green foliage, minute white flowers and a tangy, fresh smell with a pleasant, aromatic flavour. Marjoram (Origanum majorana) was considered a symbol of happiness and eternal peace for the departed soul upon whose grave it grew. It was a popular strewing herb and is an ingredient in bouquet garni. Marjoram can be used in salad dressings, and cooked in meat loaf, fish, poultry and vegetable dishes.

BOCCONCINI AND SMOKED BEEF SALAD

Bocconcini cheese is fresh baby mozzarella cheese; small mozzarella can be used. Prepare salad close to serving time. Recipe unsuitable to freeze or microwave.

12 (250g) bocconcini cheese
1 egg, lightly beaten
1 tablespoon water
½ cup plain flour
2 tablespoons chopped fresh marjoram
30g butter
1 tablespoon oil
8 slices smoked beef
1 small mignonette lettuce
250g punnet cherry tomatoes

MARJORAM DRESSING
2 tablespoons chopped fresh marjoram
2 tablespoons olive oil
1 tablespoon white wine vinegar
2 teaspoons seeded mustard

Dip bocconcini in combined egg and water. Toss in combined flour and marjoram, shake away excess flour.

Heat butter and oil in large frying

pan, add bocconcini, cook over high heat for about 2 minutes or until lightly browned; drain on absorbent paper.

Arrange bocconcini, beef, lettuce and tomatoes on plates. Pour dressing over salad just before serving.

Marjoram Dressing: Combine all ingredients in small bowl.

Serves 4.

ABOVE: Smoked Salmon and Potato Omelette. LEFT: Bocconcini and Smoked Beef Salad.

Above: Plate: Villa Italiana. Left: Plate and table: The Country Trader

SMOKED SALMON AND POTATO OMELETTE

Omelette is best made just before serving. This recipe is not suitable to freeze or microwave.

2 medium potatoes
30g butter
2 medium onions, sliced
8 eggs, lightly beaten
½ cup cream
2 tablespoons chopped fresh
 marjoram
125g smoked salmon, chopped

Cut potatoes into 1cm cubes. Heat butter in large frying pan, add onions and potatoes, stir over high heat for about 6 minutes or until potatoes are golden brown and just soft.

Combine eggs, cream and marjoram in jug, pour half the mixture evenly over onions and potatoes. Arrange salmon evenly over egg mixture, cook over low heat until omelette starts to set.

Pour remaining egg mixture over salmon, place under griller, cook until top browns slightly and omelette is set. Serve wedges of omelette with sour cream, if desired.

Serves 4.

POTATO CHOPS WITH MUSHROOM SAUCE

Crumbed chops can be prepared a day ahead; keep, covered, in refrigerator. Cook chops just before serving. Sauce is best made just before serving. Recipe unsuitable to freeze.

4 large (800g) potatoes, chopped
1 tablespoon oil
1 large onion, finely chopped
2 cloves garlic, crushed
2 teaspoons ground ginger
1 teaspoon garam masala
375g minced beef
½ cup tomato purée
1 small beef stock cube, crumbled
2 teaspoons chopped fresh coriander
2 teaspoons chopped fresh mint
2 tablespoons chopped fresh marjoram
2 eggs, lightly beaten
¼ cup milk
1 cup stale breadcrumbs
1 cup packaged breadcrumbs
oil for shallow-frying
MUSHROOM SAUCE
30g butter
4 green shallots, finely chopped
375g baby mushrooms, finely sliced
1 tablespoon brandy
2 tablespoons plain flour
1 cup milk

Boil, steam or microwave potatoes until soft, drain, mash well. Heat oil in large frying pan, add onion, garlic, ginger and garam masala, stir over medium heat for about 3 minutes (or microwave on HIGH for 4 minutes) or until onion is soft.

Add beef, stir over medium heat for about 5 minutes or until mince is browned (or microwave on HIGH for about 4 minutes); drain away fat. Stir in purée and stock cube, bring to boil, reduce heat, simmer, uncovered, for about 3 minutes (or microwave on HIGH for about 4 minutes) or until mixture is thickened.

Combine beef mixture, potato and herbs in large bowl; mix well, cover, refrigerate for several hours or overnight. Shape mixture into 12 chop shapes. Dip chops into combined eggs and milk, then combined bread-crumbs. Dip chops into egg mixture again, then breadcrumbs. Shallow-fry chops in hot oil until brown on both sides. Serve with sauce.

Mushroom Sauce: Melt butter in medium saucepan, add shallots, mushrooms and brandy, stir over low heat for about 4 minutes (or microwave

on HIGH for about 3 minutes) or until mushrooms are soft. Stir in flour, stir over medium heat for 1 minute (or microwave on HIGH for 1 minute). Remove from heat, gradually stir in milk, stir over high heat (or microwave on HIGH for about 3 minutes) until mixture boils and thickens.

Serves 6.

TOMATO JELLIES WITH SPICY TOASTS

Jellies and toasts can be made 2 days ahead; keep jellies, covered, in refrigerator. Keep toasts in airtight container. Recipe unsuitable to freeze. Toasts unsuitable to microwave.

1 tablespoon oil
1 medium onion, chopped
1 clove garlic, crushed
8 medium tomatoes (800g), peeled, seeded, chopped
1 tablespoon tomato paste
¼ teaspoon sugar
¼ teaspoon tabasco sauce
3 teaspoons chopped fresh marjoram
1½ tablespoons gelatine
¼ cup water
⅓ cup sour cream
SPICY TOASTS
2 pieces lavash or pita bread
90g butter
1 clove garlic, crushed
¼ teaspoon chilli powder
½ teaspoon paprika
¼ cup grated parmesan cheese

Lightly grease 6 moulds (½ cup capacity). Heat oil in medium frying pan, add onion and garlic, stir over medium heat for about 2 minutes (or microwave on HIGH for about 3 minutes) or until onion is soft. Add tomatoes, paste, sugar and sauce. Bring to boil, reduce heat, simmer, uncovered, for about 5 minutes (or microwave on HIGH for about 8 minutes) or until thickened slightly; stir in marjoram. Blend or process mixture until just smooth.

Sprinkle gelatine over cold water in small bowl, stand in small pan of simmering water, stir until dissolved (or microwave on HIGH for 20 seconds). Stir gelatine into tomato mixture. Spoon tomato mixture into prepared moulds. Cover, refrigerate for several hours or until firm. Turn moulds onto plates, serve with sour cream and spicy toasts.

Spicy Toasts: Cut bread into 2cm x 5cm strips. Combine butter, garlic, chilli powder and paprika in medium bowl; mix well. Dip bread strips in butter mixture, place on oven trays, sprinkle with parmesan cheese. Bake in moderate oven for about 10 minutes or until crisp; cool.

Serves 6.

RIGHT: Tomato Jellies with Spicy Toasts.
LEFT: Potato Chops with Mushroom Sauce.

Right: Plate: China Doll

CHEESY MARJORAM BREAD STICKS

Bread sticks can be made a day ahead or frozen for 2 months. Recipe unsuitable to microwave.

125g butter
2 tablespoons grated fresh
   parmesan cheese
1 tablespoon chopped fresh
   marjoram
2 tablespoons chopped fresh chives
2 teaspoons chopped fresh parsley
2 teaspoons seeded mustard
2 small French bread sticks

Beat butter with cheese, herbs and mustard in small bowl until combined. Cut bread sticks crossways at 1cm intervals, cutting nearly all the way through; spread bread slices with butter. Wrap bread sticks in foil, bake in moderate oven for about 10 minutes or until butter is melted and bread is warmed through.
   Serves 8.

LEEK PUFFS WITH MARJORAM PUMPKIN SAUCE

Unfilled puffs will keep in airtight container for a week or can be frozen for a month. Re-crisp puffs in moderate oven for 5 minutes. Fill puffs close to serving time. Puffs are unsuitable to microwave. Filling and sauce can be made a day ahead; keep, covered, in refrigerator. Filling and sauce unsuitable to freeze.

PUFFS
45g butter, chopped
½ cup water
½ cup plain flour
2 eggs, lightly beaten
LEEK FILLING
30g butter
2 medium (400g) leeks, chopped
½ cup thickened cream
1 tablespoon chopped fresh
   marjoram
MARJORAM PUMPKIN SAUCE
350g pumpkin, chopped
¾ cup water
½ large vegetable stock cube,
   crumbled
1 teaspoon cornflour
2 teaspoons water, extra
1 tablespoon chopped fresh
   marjoram

Puffs: Combine butter and water in medium saucepan, bring to boil, stirring, until butter is melted. Add flour all at once. Stir vigorously over medium heat until mixture leaves side of pan and forms a smooth ball. Place in small bowl of electric mixer (or in processor). Add eggs gradually, beat on low speed after each addition.
   Place heaped teaspoons of mixture about 5cm apart on greased oven

trays. You will need 12 puffs for this recipe. Bake in hot oven 10 minutes, reduce heat to moderate, bake further 15 minutes or until puffs are browned and well puffed. Make a small slit in side of puffs to release steam, return to moderate oven for about 10 minutes or until dry. Cool slightly, cut puffs in half, remove any doughy centre. Fill puffs and serve with sauce.

Leek Filling: Melt butter in medium saucepan, add leeks, cover, cook over low heat for about 20 minutes, stirring occasionally (or microwave on HIGH for about 8 minutes) or until leeks are soft. Blend or process leek mixture until smooth. Combine leek mixture, cream and marjoram in medium saucepan, stir over medium heat until heated through.

Marjoram Pumpkin Sauce: Boil, steam or microwave pumpkin until tender; drain. Blend or process pumpkin, water and stock cube until smooth. Blend cornflour with extra water. Combine pumpkin mixture, cornflour

mixture and marjoram in medium saucepan, stir over high heat (or microwave on HIGH for about 3 minutes) until mixture boils and thickens slightly.

Makes 12.

QUAIL EGG CANAPES

Quail eggs are available from specialty chicken shops. Herb mayonnaise can be made a day ahead; keep, covered, in refrigerator. Canapes are best made just before serving. Recipe unsuitable to freeze or microwave.

12 quail eggs
8 large slices bread
HERB MAYONNAISE
½ cup mayonnaise
2 tablespoons sour cream
1 tablespoon chopped fresh marjoram
1 teaspoon seeded mustard

Place eggs in medium saucepan, barely cover with cold water, bring to boil, stirring gently to centre yolks. Reduce heat, simmer for 4 minutes, drain, place eggs in cold water, crack shells gently, leave to cool completely.

Cut 3 rounds from each slice of bread, using 5cm cutter. Toast rounds on oven tray in moderate oven for about 3 minutes each side; cool.

Shell eggs, cut in half lengthways, cut a small slice from base of egg halves so they will sit flat. Spread each toast round with herb mayonnaise, top with egg halves. Garnish with extra marjoram leaves, if desired.

Herb Mayonnaise: Combine all ingredients in small bowl.

Makes 24.

ABOVE: Quail Egg Canapés. ABOVE LEFT: Cheesy Marjoram Bread Sticks. BELOW LEFT: Leek Puffs with Marjoram Pumpkin Sauce.

Above: Plate: Villeroy & Boch. Below left: Plates: Corso de Fiori

MINT

There are many varieties of this popular herb of Mediterranean origin. The most commonly used, spearmint (Mentha spicata), has pointed, bright green leaves and a fresh flavour. Common garden mint or green mint has rounder, coarser leaves. It was introduced to Britain by the Romans, and was a popular strewing herb to freshen the air and repel insects. Use mint in many recipes, including sweet and savoury salads, ice cream, cooked peas and mint sauce.

MINT AND APPLE JELLY

We used Granny Smith apples in this recipe. Jelly can be made 2 months ahead; keep, covered, in refrigerator. This recipe is unsuitable to freeze or microwave.

1kg medium apples
1½ litres (6 cups) water
⅓ cup lemon juice
⅓ cup chopped fresh mint
3 cups sugar, approximately
2 tablespoons chopped fresh mint, extra

Chop unpeeled apples, do not discard seeds. Combine apples, seeds, water, juice and mint in large saucepan, bring to boil, reduce heat, simmer, covered, for about 40 minutes or until apples are very soft. Strain mixture through a fine cloth into large bowl. Allow liquid to drip through cloth slowly; do not squeeze or press pulp as this will make a cloudy jelly; discard pulp.

Measure apple liquid, pour into large clean saucepan, add ¾ cup sugar to each 1 cup liquid (mixture should not be more than 5cm deep at this stage). Stir over low heat, without boiling, until sugar has dissolved, bring to boil, boil, uncovered, without stirring, for about 30 minutes or until jelly sets when tested on a cold saucer. Remove from heat, stand for 10 minutes. Stir in extra mint. Pour into hot sterilised jars; seal when cold.

Makes about 3 cups.

BELOW: Mint and Apple Jelly.

PEACHES AND MANGOES WITH MINT PASSIONFRUIT SAUCE

You need about 6 passionfruit for this recipe. Salad is best made close to serving time. Sauce can be made a day ahead; keep, covered, in refrigerator. Recipe unsuitable to freeze.

3 medium peaches, sliced
2 medium mangoes, chopped
MINT PASSIONFRUIT SAUCE
½ cup passionfruit pulp
½ cup orange juice
2 tablespoons brandy
1 tablespoon castor sugar
2 tablespoons chopped fresh mint

Arrange fruit on plate, add sauce just before serving.

Mint Passionfruit Sauce: Combine all ingredients in jar; shake well.

Serves 6.

MINTED PICNIC LOAF

Loaf can be made 2 days ahead; keep, covered, in refrigerator or freeze for 2 months. This recipe is not suitable to microwave.

1 cup stale breadcrumbs
¼ cup milk
1 medium potato, grated
250g sausage mince
250g minced beef
¼ cup tomato sauce
2 tablespoons chopped fresh mint
TOPPING
½ cup grated fresh parmesan cheese
¾ cup stale breadcrumbs
60g butter, melted
1½ tablespoons chopped fresh mint

Lightly grease 14cm x 26cm loaf pan. Combine breadcrumbs and milk in medium bowl, stand for 5 minutes. Add potato, minces, sauce and mint to breadcrumb mixture; mix well. Press mixture into prepared pan, cover with foil, bake in moderate oven 30 minutes.

Remove from oven, drain any excess liquid from pan. Press topping evenly over loaf, bake in moderate oven for about 20 minutes or until topping is golden brown. Stand loaf in pan for 15 minutes before turning out; serve warm or cold.

Topping: Combine all ingredients in medium bowl; mix well.

Serves 6.

RIGHT: Minted Picnic Loaf.
ABOVE RIGHT: Peaches and Mangoes with Mint Passionfruit Sauce.

Right: Plate: Polain Interiors. Above right: paper: House of Bambuzit

MINTED ZUCCHINI RIBBONS

Prepare close to serving time; add dressing just before serving. Dressing can be made 3 days ahead; keep, covered, in refrigerator. Recipe unsuitable to freeze.

1kg zucchini
1 medium red pepper, finely chopped
MINT DRESSING
¼ cup oil
¼ cup lemon juice
1 teaspoon sugar
3 teaspoons honey
2 tablespoons chopped fresh mint
1 teaspoon cracked black
**   peppercorns**

Using vegetable peeler, peel thin strips from zucchini. Combine zucchini and pepper in large bowl, add dressing, toss lightly.

Mint Dressing: Combine all ingredients in jar; shake well.

  Serves 6.

MINT AND TOMATO TOASTS

You can use Swiss or tasty cheese, if desired. Recipe is best prepared close to serving time. This recipe is not suitable to freeze or microwave.

12 slices white bread
3 tablespoons seeded mustard
30g butter
1 tablespoon oil
MINT AND TOMATO SAUCE
15g butter
1 medium onion, chopped
½ cup tomato purée
1 tablespoon tomato paste
½ teaspoon sugar
2 tablespoons chopped fresh mint
1 small chicken stock cube,
**   crumbled**
¼ cup water
¼ teaspoon ground cinnamon
CHEESE SAUCE
15g butter
1 clove garlic, crushed
1 tablespoon plain flour
¼ cup sweet sherry
½ cup dry white wine
1 cup grated Jarlsberg cheese

Spread 6 slices of the bread evenly with mustard, top with remaining slices, remove crusts, cut in half diagonally. Heat butter and oil in large frying pan, add sandwich triangles, cook over medium heat for about 1 minute on each side or until golden brown. Drain triangles on absorbent paper. Spread 1 side of each triangle evenly with mint and tomato sauce. Serve warm with cheese sauce.

Mint and Tomato Sauce: Melt butter in small saucepan, add onion, stir over medium heat for about 2 minutes or until onion is soft. Stir in remaining ingredients, bring to boil, reduce heat,

ingredients, bring to boil, reduce heat, simmer, uncovered, for about 10 minutes or until thickened.

Cheese Sauce: Melt butter in small saucepan, add garlic. Stir in flour, stir over medium heat 1 minute (or microwave on HIGH for 1 minute). Remove from heat, stir in sherry and wine, stir over high heat (or microwave on HIGH for about 3 minutes) or until mixture boils and thickens, reduce heat, simmer for 2 minutes (or microwave on HIGH for 2 minutes). Stir in cheese.

  Serves 6.

ABOVE: Mint and Tomato Toasts.
TOP: Minted Zucchini Ribbons.

Above: Plate: Made Where; basket: The Country Trader; napkin: Les Olivades; tiles: Country Floors. Top: plates: The Bay Tree; table: Country Form

MINT SAUCE

Mint sauce is traditionally served with roast lamb. Sauce can be made 2 weeks ahead; keep, covered, in refrigerator. Recipe unsuitable to freeze or microwave.

¾ cup cold tea
¼ cup sugar
¾ cup chopped fresh mint
½ cup white vinegar

Combine tea and sugar in small saucepan, stir over medium heat, without boiling, until sugar is dissolved. Bring to boil, remove from heat. Stir in mint and vinegar, stand for 15 minutes. Pour into sterilised bottles. Shake well before serving.

Makes about 2 cups.

SPINACH LEAF FRITTERS WITH MINT AND MANGO SAUCE

Fritters are best made close to serving time. Sauce can be made 2 days ahead; keep, covered, in refrigerator. This recipe is unsuitable to freeze or microwave.

½ cup chick pea flour
¼ cup self-raising flour
¾ cup milk
1 egg, separated
24 small English spinach leaves
oil for deep-frying
MINT AND MANGO SAUCE
1 medium mango, chopped
¼ cup macadamia nuts
2 tablespoons chopped fresh mint
2 tablespoons castor sugar

Sift flours into medium bowl, make well in centre, gradually stir in combined milk and egg yolk; mix to a smooth batter (or blend or process all ingredients until smooth). Cover, stand for 30 minutes. Beat egg white in small bowl until soft peaks form, fold into batter mixture.

Dip spinach leaves into batter, deep-fry in hot oil until puffed and golden, drain on absorbent paper; keep warm. Serve with sauce.
Mint and Mango Sauce: Blend or process all ingredients smooth.

Serves 6.

LEFT: Spinach Leaf Fritters with Mint and Mango Sauce. TOP: Mint Sauce.

Left: Serving ware: Made in Japan. Top: Jug: Burgundy Antiques; tiles: Old Balgowlah Restorations.

OREGANO

The word oregano is derived from the Greek, meaning "joy of the mountains". Oregano (Origanum vulgare) was valued as a medicinal herb in the Middle Ages. This robust relative to marjoram has firm, pungent leaves and is considered synonymous with Italian cooking. Oregano adds lusty flavour to pasta dishes, and, like basil, complements any recipe containing tomatoes. It goes well with pasta, zucchini, meat and seafood.

OREGANO HERB OIL

Herb oil can be used in salad dressings; it is best made several days before use to develop flavour. Oil can be kept refrigerated for a month. Recipe unsuitable to freeze.

750ml (3 cups) olive oil
5 sprigs fresh oregano
2 cloves garlic, peeled
8 whole black peppercorns
2 bay leaves

Pour oil into jar. Arrange oregano, garlic, peppercorns and bay leaves decoratively in oil, secure jar with lid.

Makes 3 cups.

BELOW LEFT: Oregano Herb Oil.

Table: The Country Trader; cloth: Les Olivades

PASTA MARINARA

We used fettucine in this recipe. Recipe is best made just before serving. Recipe unsuitable to freeze.

¼ cup olive oil
1 medium onion, chopped
1 clove garlic, crushed
2 x 410g cans tomatoes, drained
¼ cup dry white wine
2 teaspoons brown sugar
1 tablespoon chopped fresh oregano
1 tablespoon chopped fresh basil
250g uncooked king prawns, shelled
200g scallops
125g mussel meat
125g calamari (squid) rings
250g fresh pasta

Heat oil in medium saucepan, add onion and garlic, stir over medium heat for about 2 minutes (or microwave on HIGH for about 3 minutes) or until onion is soft.

Stir in crushed tomatoes, wine, sugar and herbs. Bring to boil, reduce heat, cover, simmer for about 10 minutes (or microwave on HIGH for about 12 minutes) or until sauce thickens slightly. Stir in seafood, simmer for about 5 minutes (or microwave on HIGH for about 3 minutes) or until tender.

Add pasta gradually to large saucepan of boiling water, boil, uncovered, until just tender; drain. Add sauce just before serving.

Serves 4.

BELOW: Pasta Marinara.

Plates: Studio Haus; table: The Country Trader

FOUR HERB BREAD

Bread is best eaten the day it is made or it can be frozen for two months. Recipe unsuitable to microwave.

7g sachet dry yeast
1 teaspoon sugar
1 cup warm milk
1 egg, lightly beaten
45g butter, melted
3¼ cups plain flour
2 tablespoons chopped fresh
   oregano
2 tablespoons chopped fresh parsley
1 tablespoon chopped fresh chives
2 teaspoons chopped fresh dill
1 egg, separated, extra
1 tablespoon milk
rock salt

Lightly grease 14cm x 21cm loaf pan. Combine yeast, sugar and milk in medium bowl, cover, stand in warm place for about 15 minutes or until foamy. Stir in egg and butter.

Sift flour into large bowl, make well in centre, gradually stir in yeast mixture, mix to a soft dough. Turn dough onto lightly floured surface, knead until smooth. Place dough into lightly oiled bowl, cover, stand in warm place for about 1 hour or until dough has doubled in size.

Knead dough on lightly floured surface for about 5 minutes or until smooth. Divide dough into 4 portions, roll 1 portion into 15cm x 20cm rectangle. Combine herbs and extra egg white in small bowl, spread quarter of the herb mixture over dough. Roll dough up from long side like a Swiss roll. Repeat with remaining dough and herb mixture.

Place 2 rolls side by side in prepared pan, top with remaining rolls. Cover, stand in warm place for about 40 minutes or until dough reaches top of pan. Brush loaf lightly with combined extra yolk and milk, sprinkle with rock salt. Bake in moderately hot oven for about 50 minutes or until golden brown and loaf sounds hollow when tapped. Stand in pan for 5 minutes before removing from pan.

LAMB OREGANO

Ask your butcher to bone the lamb for you. Recipe can be made a day ahead; keep, covered, in refrigerator; or freeze for a month. This recipe is not suitable to microwave.

30g butter
1 clove garlic, crushed
1 large onion, chopped
1 teaspoon cardamom seeds
½ teaspoon paprika
1½kg leg of lamb, boned, chopped
plain flour
425g can tomato purée
⅔ cup dry red wine
1 cup water

1 small chicken stock cube,
   crumbled
1 bay leaf
1 teaspoon sugar
2 tablesoons chopped fresh oregano

Melt butter in large saucepan, add garlic, onion, seeds and paprika, stir over medium heat for about 3 minutes or until onion is soft.

Toss lamb in flour; shake away excess flour. Add lamb gradually to pan, stir over high heat until lamb is well browned all over.

Stir in purée, wine, water, stock cube, bay leaf and sugar. Bring to boil, reduce heat, cover, simmer for about 1 hour or until meat is tender, stirring occasionally. Stir in oregano just before serving.

Serves 4.

PRAWN AND OREGANO BAKE

Recipe can be made 3 hours ahead; keep, covered, in refrigerator. Recipe unsuitable to freeze or microwave.

30g butter
1 medium leek, sliced
1 clove garlic, crushed
125g baby mushrooms, sliced
300g cooked prawns, shelled,
   chopped
1 tablespoon chopped fresh oregano
½ x 375g block puff pastry, thawed
1 egg, lightly beaten
WHITE SAUCE
2 cups milk
1 bay leaf
1 teaspoon whole black peppercorns
3 sprigs fresh oregano
30g butter
2 tablespoons plain flour

Melt butter in medium frying pan, add leek, garlic and mushrooms, stir over low heat for about 5 minutes or until leek is soft. Stir in prawns, oregano and white sauce. Spoon mixture into 4 ovenproof dishes (¾ cup capacity).

Roll pastry large enough to cut 4 rounds to cover tops of dishes. Brush edges of rounds lightly with egg, place over dishes, press edges firmly onto dishes. Decorate with extra pastry, brush with egg, bake in hot oven about 10 minutes or until golden brown.

White Sauce: Place milk, bay leaf, peppercorns and oregano in small saucepan, bring to boil, remove from heat, cover, stand 10 minutes; strain.

Melt butter in small saucepan, stir in flour, stir over medium heat for 1 minute (or microwave on HIGH for 1 minute). Gradually stir in strained milk, stir over high heat (or microwave on HIGH for about 4 minutes) until sauce boils and thickens.

Serves 4.

ABOVE LEFT: Four Herb Bread. BELOW LEFT: Lamb Oregano. BELOW: Prawn and Oregano Bake.

Above left: Setting: Appley Hoare Antiques. Below: Pot: The Bay Tree; plate: Home & Garden; bowl: Whitehouse; cloth: Les Olivades. Below left: Rug: Les Olivades.

PASTA WITH SUN-DRIED TOMATOES AND SALAMI

We used fresh tagliatelle in this recipe. You will need to buy 300g fresh pasta or 175g dried pasta. Sauce can be made a day ahead; keep, covered, in refrigerator. Recipe unsuitable to freeze or microwave.

30g butter
2 tablespoons chopped fresh
**   oregano**
2 green shallots, chopped
2 small fresh red chillies, chopped
300g jar sun-dried tomatoes
200g can pimientos, drained
1 cup water
2 teaspoons oil
500g hot salami, chopped
300g fresh pasta

Melt butter in medium saucepan, add oregano, shallots and chillies, stir over medium heat for about 2 minutes (or microwave on HIGH for about 2 minutes) or until shallots are soft.

Blend or process shallot mixture, undrained tomatoes and pimientos until smooth. Add water gradually in thin stream while motor is operating, blend or process until combined. Return mixture to same pan, stir over low heat until warm.

Heat oil in medium frying pan, add salami, stir over high heat for about 5 minutes or until salami is slightly crisp, drain on absorbent paper. Stir salami into tomato sauce, stir over medium heat until heated through.

Add pasta gradually to large saucepan of boiling water, boil, uncovered, until just tender; drain. Combine with sauce before serving.
Serves 4.

OAT-COATED SMOKED CHEESE WITH OREGANO VINAIGRETTE

Cheese can be coated a day ahead; keep, covered, in refrigerator. Recipe unsuitable to freeze or microwave.

200g smoked cheese
plain flour
1 egg, lightly beaten
1 tablespoon milk
¾ cup rolled oats
60g butter
2 tablespoons oil
OREGANO VINAIGRETTE
¼ cup olive oil
2 teaspoons white vinegar
3 teaspoons lemon juice
1 small clove garlic, crushed
2 teaspoons chopped fresh oregano

Cut cheese into 1cm slices, cut slices into quarters. Dust cheese with flour, dip in combined egg and milk, then toss in oats. Dip in egg mixture again, then oats.

Heat butter and oil in large frying

pan, add cheese in single layer, cook over medium heat until oats are brown all over; drain on absorbent paper. Serve with oregano vinaigrette.
Oregano Vinaigrette: Blend or process all ingredients until combined.
Serves 4.

ABOVE: Oat-Coated Smoked Cheese with Oregano Vinaigrette. TOP: Pasta with Sun-Dried Tomatoes and Salami.

Above: Plate: The Country Trader

PARSLEY

There are two varieties of this versatile herb, curled parsley, with its well-known bright green frills of foliage, and Italian parsley, which has larger, flatter leaves and a mild celery flavour. The Greeks used parsley (Petroselinum crispum) as horse fodder and as a garlanding herb. Charlemagne, the ninth century emperor, was fond of cheese flavoured with parsley seeds. Parsley is a universal garnish and blends well with other herbs and seasonings.

APRICOT CHICKEN TERRINE

Terrine can be made 2 days ahead; keep, covered, in refrigerator. Recipe unsuitable to freeze or microwave.

1 cup chopped dried apricots
½ cup water
¼ cup olive oil
1 large onion, finely chopped
1 cup stale breadcrumbs
¼ cup chopped fresh parsley
2 tablespoons chopped fresh chives
1 egg
1½kg chicken breast fillets, chopped
¾ cup stale breadcrumbs, extra
1 teaspoon ground coriander
3 tablespoons gelatine
¾ cup water, extra
2 teaspoons grated lemon rind
¼ cup lemon juice

Lightly grease 14cm x 21cm loaf dish. Place apricots and water in small bowl, cover, stand for 30 minutes.

Heat oil in small frying pan, add onion, stir over medium heat for about 3 minutes or until onion is soft. Combine undrained apricots, onion mixture, breadcrumbs, parsley, chives and egg in medium bowl; mix well. Blend or process chicken until smooth. Combine chicken, extra breadcrumbs and coriander in medium bowl, mix well.

Spread one-third of the chicken mixture into prepared dish, top with half the apricot mixture. Repeat layering, ending with chicken layer. Cover dish with foil, bake in moderate oven for about 1 hour or until set. Drain any liquid from terrine; cool in dish.

Sprinkle gelatine over extra water in small bowl, stand in small saucepan of simmering water, stir until dissolved. Stir in rind and juice. Pour gelatine mixture over terrine in dish, refrigerate until set before turning out.

Serves 8.

LEFT: Apricot Chicken Terrine.

Left: Plate and tea-towel: The Bay Tree; box: Appley Hoare Antiques

PARSLEY CRUMBED VEAL

Veal can be crumbed several hours ahead; keep, covered, in refrigerator. This recipe is not suitable to freeze or microwave.

8 small veal steaks
150g Jarlsberg or Swiss cheese, sliced
plain flour
1 egg, lightly beaten
2 tablespoons milk
1 cup packaged breadcrumbs
¼ cup chopped fresh parsley
1 teaspoon grated lemon or lime rind
60g butter
2 tablespoons oil

Pound steaks thinly, place cheese over half the steaks, top with remaining steaks. Pound edges together to enclose cheese. Coat steaks lightly in flour, shake away excess flour, dip in combined egg and milk, then coat firmly with combined breadcrumbs, parsley and rind.

Heat butter and oil in large frying pan, add steaks, cook over medium heat for about 2 minutes on each side or until golden brown and tender. Remove steaks from pan, drain on absorbent paper.

Serves 4.

PARSLEY AND MUSTARD CRUSTED LAMB RACKS

Recipe can be prepared a day ahead; keep, covered, in refrigerator. Recipe unsuitable to freeze or microwave.

4 racks of lamb (4 cutlets each)
CRUST
2 cloves garlic, crushed
4 green shallots, chopped
½ cup chopped fresh parsley
2 tablespoons chopped fresh sage
⅓ cup seeded mustard
½ cup stale breadcrumbs
⅓ cup olive oil
2 tablespoons lemon juice

Trim excess fat from racks, cover bones with foil. Press crust mixture evenly onto back of each rack, cover, refrigerate for several hours. Place lamb on rack in baking dish, bake in moderately hot oven for about 20 minutes or until tender.

Crust: Combine all ingredients in small bowl; mix well.

Serves 4.

PARSLEY AND BACON PASTA

We used fettucine pasta in this recipe. Recipe is best prepared close to serving time. This recipe is unsuitable to freeze.

375g pasta
30g butter
1 medium onion, thinly sliced
4 bacon rashers, chopped
¾ cup cream
1 egg, lightly beaten
¼ cup chopped fresh parsley

Add pasta gradually to large saucepan of boiling water, boil, uncovered, until just tender, drain.

Melt butter in large frying pan, add onion and bacon, stir over high heat for

about 2 minutes (or microwave on HIGH for about 3 minutes) or until onion is soft. Stir in combined cream, egg and parsley, stir over low heat for about 2 minutes (or microwave on HIGH for about 2 minutes) or until mixture thickens slightly; do not allow to boil. Stir in pasta, stir over medium heat (or microwave on HIGH for about 1 minute) until heated through.

Serves 4.

ABOVE: Parsley Crumbed Veal. TOP RIGHT: Parsley and Mustard Crusted Lamb Racks. RIGHT: Parsley and Bacon Pasta.

Above: Plates: The Bay Tree; cloth and food cover: Appley Hoare Antiques

SAUCY BABY SQUASH
WITH SALAMI

Recipe is best prepared close to serving time. This recipe is unsuitable to freeze.

1 tablespoon oil
1 medium onion, sliced
1 clove garlic, crushed
500g baby squash
425g can tomatoes, drained
1 tablespoon tomato paste
2 tablespoons chopped fresh
   flat-leafed parsley
200g pepperoni salami, thinly sliced

Heat oil in medium saucepan, add onion and garlic, stir over medium heat for about 2 minutes (or microwave on HIGH for about 3 minutes) or until onion is soft. Stir in squash, crushed tomatoes, paste and half the parsley. Cover, cook over medium heat for about 5 minutes (or microwave on HIGH for about 6 minutes) or until squash are tender.

Cook salami in medium frying pan over medium heat until crisp, drain on absorbent paper. Add salami to squash mixture, toss well, serve sprinkled with remaining parsley.

Serves 4.

BAKED FISH
WITH PARSLEY SEASONING

Fish can be prepared 3 hours ahead; keep, covered, in refrigerator. Bake just before serving. Recipe unsuitable to freeze or microwave.

90g butter
1 clove garlic, crushed
1 medium onion, chopped
125g baby mushrooms, sliced
1 bacon rasher, chopped
1½ cups (150g) stale breadcrumbs
2 tablespoons lemon juice
⅓ cup chopped fresh parsley
2 x 750g whole snapper
¼ cup lemon juice, extra
2 tablespoons water

Melt butter in large frying pan, add garlic and onion, stir over medium heat for about 2 minutes or until onion is soft. Stir in mushrooms and bacon, stir over medium heat for about 3 minutes or until mushrooms are soft. Remove pan from heat, stir in breadcrumbs, juice and parsley.

Spoon seasoning into fish. Place fish in single layer in large baking dish, sprinkle with extra lemon juice and water, cover, bake in moderate oven for about 40 minutes or until tender.

Serves 4.

ABOVE LEFT: Saucy Baby Squash with Salami. LEFT: Baked Fish with Parsley Seasoning.

Above left: Plate: Made in Japan. Left: Plate: Burgundy Antiques

ROSEMARY

Rosemary (Rosmarinus officinalis) has dark green, firm narrow leaves with a fresh piney fragrance and a warm, savoury taste. This compact evergreen shrub has mauvey-blue flowers, and legend says that the Virgin Mary, while resting, spread her cloak over a white-flowering rosemary bush. The flowers turned the blue of her cloak, and from then on the bush was referred to as "Rose of Mary". Greek scholars wore rosemary in their hair to help remember their studies, and the association with remembrance is carried through to today, when rosemary is worn on Anzac Day.

LAMB WITH ROSEMARY TOPPING

Lamb can be prepared 2 days ahead; keep, covered, in refrigerator. Cook just before serving. Recipe unsuitable to freeze or microwave.

2kg leg of lamb
4 cloves garlic, sliced
⅓ cup olive oil
1 teaspoon grated lemon rind
⅓ cup lemon juice
1 tablespoon tomato paste
2 teaspoons cracked black peppercorns
1½ tablespoons seeded mustard
1 teaspoon sugar
2 teaspoons chopped fresh thyme
¼ cup chopped fresh rosemary

Using sharp knife, make small incisions in the lamb, insert a slice of garlic into each incision. Place lamb in large baking dish.

Combine oil, rind, juice, paste, peppercorns, mustard and sugar in medium bowl; whisk until mixture thickens. Brush lamb with one-third of the oil mixture, bake in moderate oven for 10 minutes. Brush lamb with half the remaining oil mixture, bake further 10 minutes. Brush lamb with remaining oil mixture, sprinkle with thyme, bake in moderately slow oven for 1 hour. Sprinkle lamb with rosemary, bake further 15 minutes or until lamb is tender.

Serves 6.

ABOVE: Lamb with Rosemary Topping.

ROSEMARY RISOTTO

Risotto is best made just before serving. Risotto unsuitable to freeze.

60g butter
1 medium onion, chopped
2 sticks celery, chopped
2 tablespoons chopped fresh rosemary
1 cup rice
½ cup dry white wine
2½ cups hot water
1 large vegetable stock cube, crumbled
tiny pinch saffron powder
½ cup fresh or frozen peas
¼ cup grated fresh parmesan cheese

Melt butter in large frying pan, add onion, celery and rosemary, stir over medium heat for about 3 minutes (or microwave on HIGH for about 4 minutes) or until onion is soft.

Stir in rice, stir until rice is well coated with butter. Stir in wine, 1 cup of the hot water, stock cube and saffron, bring to boil, reduce heat, simmer, uncovered, for about 10 minutes (or microwave on HIGH for about 10 minutes) or until most of the liquid has been absorbed, stir occasionally during cooking.

Add remaining hot water and peas, simmer, uncovered, further 10 minutes (or microwave on HIGH for about 15 minutes) or until all the liquid has been absorbed. Remove from heat, stir in cheese.

Serves 4.

PUMPKIN AND ZUCCHINI WITH ROSEMARY

Vegetables are best prepared close to serving time. This recipe is not suitable to freeze.

2 medium zucchini
350g pumpkin
15g butter
2 bacon rashers, sliced
3 teaspoons chopped fresh rosemary

Cut zucchini and pumpkin into thin sticks. Boil, steam or microwave zucchini and pumpkin until just tender; drain. Melt butter in medium saucepan, add bacon, stir over medium heat (or microwave on HIGH for about 1 minute) or until bacon is starting to crisp. Add rosemary, zucchini and pumpkin, toss lightly to combine.

Serves 4.

RIGHT: Rosemary Butter.
FAR RIGHT: From top: Rosemary Risotto; Pumpkin and Zucchini with Rosemary; Veal Chops with Rosemary Sauce.

Far right: Terracotta: Villa Italiana; chair and cabinet: The Country Trader

VEAL CHOPS WITH ROSEMARY SAUCE

Recipe is best prepared just before serving. This recipe is not suitable to freeze or microwave.

8 small veal chops
30g butter
1 tablespoon oil
2 tablespoons chopped fresh rosemary
2 teaspoons cornflour
1 tablespoon brandy
¾ cup water
½ small beef stock cube, crumbled
1 teaspoon sugar

Trim tail from each chop. Heat butter and oil in large frying pan, add rosemary, stir over medium heat for 1 minute. Add chops, cook over medium heat for about 3 minutes on each side or until tender. Remove chops from pan; keep warm.

Blend cornflour with brandy, water, stock cube and sugar, stir into pan, stir over high heat until mixture boils and thickens. Serve sauce over chops.

Serves 4.

ROSEMARY BUTTER

Serve butter with lamb, beef or chicken. Butter can be made 2 days ahead; keep, covered, in refrigerator. Butter can be frozen for 2 months.

125g butter
1 tablespoon chopped fresh rosemary
½ teaspoon cracked black peppercorns
2 teaspoons grated orange rind

Place all ingredients in small bowl of electric mixer; beat until combined. Spoon mixture onto a sheet of greaseproof paper, shape into a roll 4cm in diameter, roll in paper, twist ends of paper to secure. Refrigerate until firm.

ROSEMARY DAMPER

Damper is best served hot with butter. Cooked damper can be frozen for 2 months. This recipe is not suitable to microwave.

15g butter
1 medium onion, chopped
3 bacon rashers, chopped
3 cups self-raising flour
45g butter, extra
2 tablespoons chopped fresh rosemary
1 cup grated tasty cheese
½ cup milk
¾ cup water, approximately

Melt butter in small frying pan, add onion and bacon, stir over medium heat for about 2 minutes or until onion is soft; cool.

Sift flour into large bowl, rub in extra butter. Stir in onion mixture, rosemary and ⅔ cup of the cheese, make well in centre. Stir in milk and enough water to mix to a soft dough. Knead on lightly floured surface until smooth.

Place dough onto greased oven tray, pat into 16cm circle. Using sharp knife, cut a cross into top of dough about 1cm deep. Brush with a little extra milk, sprinkle with remaining cheese. Bake in moderate oven for about 40 minutes or until damper is golden brown and sounds hollow when tapped with finger.

ABOVE: Rosemary Damper.

Above: Plate and bowl: Corso de Fiori; ceramic stand and tray: Duane Norris, garden designers.

SAGE

The greenish-grey, long leaves of sage (Salvia officinalis) have a savoury, dry aroma and a somewhat spicy flavour that is a natural counter-balance for rich and fatty foods. Sage was believed to prolong life in Roman times, when it was a medicinal herb. The grainy-textured leaves were popular with the Chinese during the 17th century, and are considered a traditional seasoning in stuffings for pork and game.

HONEY AND LEMON SPATCHCOCKS

Spatchcocks can be prepared a day ahead; keep, covered, in refrigerator. Bake spatchcocks just before serving. This recipe is not suitable to freeze or microwave.

4 x size 4 spatchcocks
15g butter
1 tablespoon honey
1 tablespoon lemon juice
½ cup water
1 tablespoon cornflour
1 tablespoon water, extra
1 tablespoon chopped fresh sage

SAGE SEASONING
30g butter
1 medium (200g) leek, finely chopped
2 bacon rashers, finely chopped
1 tablespoon chopped fresh sage
1 egg, lightly beaten
½ cup ground hazelnuts
Spoon seasoning into spatchcocks; secure openings with toothpicks, tie legs together with string.

Combine butter, honey, juice and water in medium baking dish, stir over heat until butter is melted. Place spatchcocks in dish, bake in moderate oven for about 1 hour, basting occasionally with pan juices, or until spatchcocks are tender. Remove spatchcocks from dish, keep warm.

Blend cornflour with extra water and sage, stir into dish, stir over high heat until sauce boils and thickens. Remove string, pour sauce over spatchcocks just before serving.

Sage Seasoning: Melt butter in medium saucepan, add leek and bacon, stir over medium heat for about 5 minutes or until leek is soft, cool. Stir in sage, egg and hazelnuts.

Serves 4.

ABOVE: Honey and Lemon Spatchcocks.

99

SAGE POTATOES

Potatoes are best prepared just before serving. Recipe unsuitable to freeze or microwave.

60g butter
1 tablespoon chopped fresh sage
5 large (1kg) potatoes, chopped
½ cup grated tasty cheese

Melt butter in medium frying pan, add sage and potatoes, stir over medium heat for about 3 minutes or until potatoes are golden; transfer to shallow ovenproof dish (3 cup capacity). Sprinkle cheese over potatoes, bake in moderately hot oven for about 45 minutes or until potatoes are tender.

Serves 4.

LAMB'S FRY WITH SAGE

Recipe is best made just before serving. Recipe unsuitable to freeze or microwave.

1 lamb's fry (about 500g)
¼ cup plain flour
2 tablespoons chopped fresh sage
30g butter
2 tablespoons oil
1 clove garlic, crushed
1 medium green pepper, sliced
¼ cup dry sherry
1 teaspoon cornflour
½ cup water
⅓ cup cream
1 small beef stock cube, crumbled
1 tablespoon chopped fresh sage, extra

Soak lamb's fry in bowl of salted cold water for 1 hour, drain. Remove skin, using sharp knife; cut fry into thin slices. Toss fry in combined flour and sage, shake away excess flour.

Heat butter and oil in large frying pan, add fry, cook over medium heat for about 4 minutes or until lightly browned on both sides and tender. Remove fry from pan, drain on absorbent paper.

Add garlic and pepper to pan, stir over medium heat for about 3 minutes or until pepper is just tender. Stir in sherry, simmer for 1 minute.

Blend cornflour with water, cream, stock cube and extra sage, stir into pepper mixture, stir over high heat until sauce boils and thickens slightly. Return fry to pan, reduce heat, simmer, uncovered, for 2 minutes.

Serves 4.

LEFT: From top: Sage Potatoes; Lamb's Fry with Sage. ABOVE: Sausage, Sage and Apple Plait.

SAUSAGE, SAGE AND APPLE PLAIT

Recipe can be made 2 days ahead; keep, covered, in refrigerator. Recipe unsuitable to freeze or microwave.

375g packet frozen puff pastry, thawed
1 egg, lightly beaten
FILLING
250g sausage mince
1 large onion, chopped
1 large apple, chopped
2 tablespoons chopped fresh sage
1 egg, lightly beaten

Lightly grease oven tray. Roll pastry on lightly floured surface into 25cm x 30cm rectangle; trim edges. Transfer pastry to oven tray, spoon filling down centre of pastry, leaving 10 cm border on long sides. Cut pastry diagonally at 2cm intervals down each side of filling, criss-cross the strips of pastry across filling like a plait. Brush pastry with egg.

Bake plait in moderate oven for about 40 minutes or until golden brown and cooked through. Stand 5 minutes before cutting. Serve hot or cold.

Filling: Combine all ingredients in medium bowl; mix well.

Serves 6.

SAVORY

Both winter (Saturea montana) and summer (Saturea hortensis) savory are popular herbs with a piquant, slightly peppery flavour. Savory was once thought to be an aphrodisiac, and was used in food 2000 year ago. The Germans call it "bean herb" and use it often with green and dried beans. Savory goes well with all kinds of cooked beans, enhances poultry, veal and seafood, and can be used as a mild substitute for pepper.

LAMB AND SAVORY CASSEROLE

Casserole can be prepared 2 days ahead; keep, covered, in refrigerator or freeze for 2 months. Casserole unsuitable to microwave.

1kg lamb leg chops
¼ cup oil
2 medium onions, quartered
2 cloves garlic, crushed
4 medium zucchini, sliced
½ cup tomato paste
1 small beef stock cube, crumbled
1 cup water
1 cup dry white wine
1½ tablespoons chopped fresh savory
1 tablespoon chopped fresh marjoram

Remove fat and bones from chops; cut lamb into 2cm cubes. Heat half the oil in large saucepan, add lamb, stir over medium heat for about 7 minutes or until lamb is well browned. Remove from heat, drain on absorbent paper.

Heat remaining oil in same pan, add onions and garlic, stir over medium heat for about 3 minutes or until onions are soft. Stir in lamb and remaining ingredients, bring to boil, reduce heat, cover, simmer for about 30 minutes or until lamb is tender; stir occasionally.

Serves 4.

HONEY AND ORANGE GLAZED DRUMSTICKS

Recipe can be made a day ahead; keep, covered in refrigerator or freeze for 2 months.

1 tablespoon chopped fresh savory
3 teaspoons chopped fresh marjoram
¼ cup honey
½ cup orange juice
2 teaspoons light soy sauce

2 teaspoons oil
8 chicken drumsticks
2 teaspoons cornflour
2 teaspoons water

Combine herbs, honey, juice, sauce and oil in large bowl, add chicken, stir to coat with marinade. Cover, refrigerate for 2 hours. Place chicken in baking dish, reserve marinade. Bake in moderate oven for about 45 minutes (or microwave on HIGH for about 18 minutes) or until chicken is tender,

brush occasionally with marinade. Remove chicken from dish; keep warm.

Add remaining marinade to dish. Blend cornflour with water, stir into dish, stir over HIGH heat (or microwave on HIGH for about 3 minutes) until mixture boils and thickens slightly.

Serves 4.

LEFT: Lamb and Savory Casserole.
ABOVE: Honey and Orange Glazed Drumsticks.

Left: Casserole pot: Village Living. Above: Plate: Hampshire & Lowndes; pots: Made Where; bucket: The Country Trader

CRAB PATTIES WITH SPICY TOMATO SAUCE

Uncooked patties can be prepared a day ahead; keep, covered, in refrigerator. Sauce can be made 3 hours ahead; keep, covered, in refrigerator. This recipe is unsuitable to freeze or microwave.

2 x 200g cans crab meat, drained
½ cup sour cream
1 egg, lightly beaten

2 green shallots, finely chopped
2 cups (200g) stale breadcrumbs
1 tablespoon Worcestershire sauce
½ small green pepper, finely chopped
1½ tablespoons chopped fresh marjoram
1 tablespoon chopped fresh savory
1 cup stale breadcrumbs, extra
½ cup grated parmesan cheese
2 tablespoons chopped fresh savory, extra

2 cloves garlic, crushed
½ teaspoon cayenne pepper
¼ cup oil
SPICY TOMATO SAUCE
15g butter
1 medium onion, chopped
1 small green pepper, finely chopped
1 cup water
1 small chicken stock cube, crumbled
410g can tomatoes
½ teaspoon tabasco sauce

1 tablespoon chopped fresh savory
2 teaspoons cornflour
1 tablespoon water, extra

Combine crab, cream, egg, shallots, breadcrumbs, sauce, pepper, marjoram and savory in medium bowl; mix well. Shape mixture into 8 patties, toss in combined extra breadcrumbs, cheese, extra savory, garlic and pepper. Place patties on tray, cover, refrigerate for several hours.

Heat oil in large frying pan, add patties a few at a time, cook over medium heat for about 4 minutes or until browned on each side, drain on absorbent paper. Repeat with remaining patties. Serve patties with warm spicy tomato sauce.

Spicy Tomato Sauce: Melt butter in medium saucepan, add onion and pepper, stir over medium heat for about 2 minutes or until pepper is soft. Stir in water, stock cube, undrained crushed tomatoes, sauce and savory.

Bring to the boil, reduce heat, simmer, uncovered, for 15 minutes. Stir in blended cornflour and extra water, stir over high heat until sauce boils and thickens.

Serves 4.

POTATO AND KUMARA BAKE

Kumara is an orange coloured sweet potato. Bake can be made a day ahead; keep, covered, in refrigerator. Recipe unsuitable to freeze.

4 bacon rashers, chopped
10 green shallots, chopped
4 large (1kg) potatoes
2 large (750g) kumara
1 large carrot
2 tablespoons oil
1½ teaspoons fennel seeds
2 tablespoons plain flour
300ml carton thickened cream
2 tablespoons chopped fresh savory
TOPPING
2 teaspoons oil
4 bacon rashers, chopped
1½ cups (150g) stale breadcrumbs
300ml carton thickened cream
2 tablespoons chopped fresh savory
2 tablespoons chopped fresh parsley
90g butter, melted

Combine bacon and shallots in medium frying pan, stir over medium heat for about 3 minutes (or microwave on HIGH for about 2 minutes) or until shallots are soft; drain on absorbent paper. Cut potatoes, kumara and carrot into thin sticks.

Heat oil in large frying pan, add potatoes, stir over medium heat for 4 minutes, stir in kumara and carrot, stir over medium heat for about 5 minutes (or microwave on HIGH for about 6 minutes) or until vegetables are just soft. Remove from heat, stir in seeds, flour, cream and savory.

Spoon mixture into large shallow ovenproof dish (10 cup capacity). Spread with topping. Bake in moderate oven for about 40 minutes or until lightly browned and crisp (or microwave on HIGH for about 20 minutes).

Topping: Heat oil in medium frying pan, add bacon, stir over medium heat for about 3 minutes (or microwave on HIGH for about 2 minutes) or until bacon is browned. Remove from heat, stir in breadcrumbs, cream, savory, parsley and butter.

Serves 8.

LEFT: Crab Patties with Spicy Tomato Sauce. BELOW: Potato and Kumara Bake.

Left: Plate: Hampshire & Lowndes: tiles: Country Floors.
Below: Oven baker: Polain Interiors

SORREL

French sorrel (Rumex scutatus) grows in clumps similar to spinach. The young leaves of this hardy annual give a hint of lemon flavour, and mature to impart a bitter, slightly sour taste. In Egyptian times, sorrel was eaten to offset the richness of some foods. Cook and eat sorrel like spinach, in soup and white sauces to accompany poultry, fish and potatoes. Like spinach, sorrel should not be cooked in aluminium.

SORREL AND QUAIL EGG SALAD

Quail eggs are available at specialty chicken shops. Salad can be made 3 hours ahead; keep, covered, in refrigerator. Add dressing just before serving. Recipe unsuitable to freeze or microwave.

6 quail eggs
2 slices white bread
30g butter
1 bunch (10 spears) asparagus, chopped
125g baby mushrooms, sliced
1 small red pepper, sliced
50g pastrami, sliced
10 sorrel leaves, shredded
¼ bunch curly endive
DRESSING
¼ cup mayonnaise
¼ cup sour light cream
1 tablespoon lemon juice
1 tablespoon chopped fresh sorrel

Place eggs in small saucepan, barely cover with cold water, bring to boil, stirring gently so yolks will be centred. Reduce heat, simmer for 4 minutes, drain, place in cold water to cool completely. Shell eggs, cut in half.

Remove crusts from bread, cut bread into cubes. Heat butter in small frying pan, add bread cubes, toss over medium heat until cubes are golden brown; remove from heat. Boil, steam or microwave asparagus until just tender; drain.

Arrange eggs, bread cubes, asparagus and remaining ingredients on plate, add dressing before serving.
Dressing: Combine all ingredients in small bowl, stir well.
Serves 4.

CHICKEN QUENELLES WITH CREAMY SORREL SAUCE

Quenelle mixture and sauce can be prepared a day ahead; keep, covered, in refrigerator. Cook quenelles just before serving. Recipe unsuitable to freeze or microwave.

500g chicken breast fillets, chopped
3 egg whites
½ cup sour cream
½ cup chopped fresh sorrel
2 cups water
½ cup dry white wine
2 small chicken stock cubes, crumbled
CREAMY SORREL SAUCE
3 egg yolks
2 teaspoons seeded mustard
1 tablespoon redcurrant jelly
⅔ cup cream
½ cup chopped fresh sorrel

Blend or process fillets, egg whites, cream and sorrel until smooth and creamy. Place mixture in medium bowl, cover, refrigerate for 1 hour. Combine water, wine and stock cubes in large frying pan, bring to boil, reduce heat so liquid is simmering.

LEFT: Sorrel and Quail Egg Salad.
RIGHT: Chicken Quenelles with Creamy Sorrel Sauce.

Left: Plate: Village Living. Right: Tray: Corso de Fiori

Using 2 wet dessertspoons, mould mixture into oval shapes. Place ovals carefully into the simmering liquid, poach for about 2 minutes on each side. Do not allow water to boil or quenelles will fall apart. Drain on absorbent paper, serve with sauce.

Creamy Sorrel Sauce: Whisk egg yolks and mustard in medium bowl until thick and creamy. Combine jelly and cream in small saucepan, stir over medium heat until almost boiling. Pour mixture over yolks, whisking constantly. Stir in sorrel. Place bowl over pan of simmering water, stir until sauce thickens slightly.

Serves 6.

VEAL AND SORREL ROLLS

Rolls can be prepared 2 days ahead; keep, covered, in refrigerator or freeze for 2 months. Bake rolls just before serving. This recipe is unsuitable to microwave.

4 large veal steaks
plain flour
2 teaspoons oil
2 teaspoons butter
1 tablespoon plain flour, extra
2 tablespoons sweet sherry
¾ cup water
1 small beef stock cube, crumbled
2 teaspoons Worcestershire sauce
2 tablespoons cream
1 tablespoon chopped fresh sorrel

BRAISED LEEK
1 medium (200g) leek
30g butter

SORREL AND BACON SEASONING
1 tablespoon oil
1 medium onion, finely chopped
1 bacon rasher, finely chopped
1 clove garlic, crushed
90g chicken livers, chopped
1 tablespoon chopped walnuts
½ cup stale breadcrumbs
1 tablespoon chopped fresh sorrel

Pound each steak until about 12cm x 15cm; trim edges. Place a quarter of the seasoning onto narrow end of each steak, roll up like a Swiss roll; secure with toothpicks. Toss rolls in flour, shake away excess flour.

Heat oil and butter in medium frying pan, add rolls, cook over medium heat for about 5 minutes or until browned all over. Place rolls into medium ovenproof dish.

Stir extra flour into pan, stir over medium heat for about 2 minutes or until golden brown. Remove from heat, gradually stir in combined sherry, water, stock cube and sauce. Stir over high heat until mixture boils and thickens, pour over rolls; cover, bake in moderate oven for 45 minutes, turning rolls once. Remove rolls from liquid, keep warm.

Strain liquid into small saucepan, stir in cream, stir over medium heat until mixture boils, remove from heat, stir in sorrel. Remove toothpicks from rolls, cut rolls into slices, serve with braised leek and sauce.

Braised Leek: Wash leek well, cut into thin strips. Melt butter in large frying pan, add leek, stir over medium heat for about 5 minutes or until leek is soft.

Sorrel and Bacon Seasoning: Heat oil in medium frying pan, add onion, bacon and garlic, stir over medium heat for about 2 minutes or until onion is soft. Add livers, stir over medium heat for about 2 minutes or until cooked through. Place mixture into medium bowl, stir in walnuts, breadcrumbs and sorrel.

Serves 4.

SORREL AND WONTON SOUP

Wontons can be prepared several hours ahead; keep, covered, in refrigerator or freeze for 2 months. Soup is best made just before serving.

1 medium carrot
2 litres (8 cups) water
2 large chicken stock cubes,
   crumbled
½ teaspoon sesame oil
375g broccoli, chopped
1 bunch fresh sorrel, shredded
WONTONS
25g Chinese dried mushrooms
125g pork and veal mince
½ cup finely chopped cabbage
130g can creamed corn

1 green shallot, finely chopped
1 teaspoon light soy sauce
2 tablespoons chopped fresh sorrel
¼ teaspoon sesame oil
3 teaspoons grated fresh ginger
32 wonton wrappers
1 egg, lightly beaten
Cut carrot into thin sticks. Bring water to boil in large saucepan, stir in stock cubes, oil, broccoli and carrot, boil, uncovered, for about 5 minutes or until vegetables are tender. Stir in sorrel. Place warm wontons into serving bowls, top with soup.

Wontons: Cover mushrooms with hot water, stand for 10 minutes; drain, discard stems; chop finely. Combine mushrooms, mince, cabbage, corn, shallot, sauce, sorrel, oil and ginger in small bowl; mix well. Top each wrapper with a heaped teaspoon of mince mixture, brush edges with egg, pull edges together to form a pouch. Drop wontons into large saucepan of boiling water, boil, uncovered, for about 5 minutes, or until cooked through; drain.

Serves 6.

ABOVE LEFT: Veal and Sorrel Rolls.
ABOVE: Sorrel and Wonton Soup.

Above left: Plate: Villa Italiana; knife and spoon: Appley Hoare Antiques; lace: Laura Ashley. Above: Tray, bowl and scarf: Made in Japan

SORREL GNOCCHI
WITH PIMIENTO SAUCE

Gnocchi is best cooked just before serving. Sauce can be made 3 days ahead; keep, covered, in refrigerator. Sauce and uncooked gnocchi can be frozen for 3 months. Gnocchi unsuitable to microwave.

5 medium (500g) old potatoes
2 tablespoons chopped fresh sorrel
1½ cups plain flour
¾ cup grated fresh parmesan cheese
PIMIENTO SAUCE
1 tablespoon olive oil
1 medium onion, chopped
2 cloves garlic, crushed
400g can pimientos, drained, chopped
¼ cup tomato paste
1 cup water

1 small chicken stock cube, crumbled
½ cup dry white wine
1 tablespoon chopped fresh sorrel

Boil, steam or microwave potatoes until soft; drain. Press potatoes through sieve into large bowl, add sorrel; mix well. Knead in sifted flour, a quarter cup at a time. Knead dough on lightly floured surface until smooth. Shape mixture into approximately 1½cm balls.

Place a ball of mixture into palm of hand, press floured prongs of fork on top of ball to make an indentation, as pictured. Repeat with remaining balls.

Add gnocchi to large saucepan of boiling water, boil for about 2 minutes or until gnocchi floats to the surface, drain; keep warm. Serve gnocchi warm with sauce, sprinkled with cheese.

Pimiento Sauce: Heat oil in medium saucepan, add onion and garlic, stir over medium heat for about 2 minutes (or microwave on HIGH for about 3 minutes) or until onion is soft. Stir in remaining ingredients, bring to boil, reduce heat, cover, simmer for about 10 minutes (or microwave on HIGH for about 15 minutes) or until sauce thickens slightly.

Serves 6.

TARRAGON

French tarragon (Artemesia dracunculus) has straight, smooth, narrow leaves growing from a tangle of stems. It is thought that the French name "estragon" or "little dragon" refers to its reputation for curing reptile bites or to its coiled, serpent-like roots. Tarragon has a unique tart flavour and piquant aroma, making it a highly sought-after gourmet's herb. Use in bearnaise and tartare sauces, add to chicken, game and turkey. Steep a whole sprig in vinegar for making salad dressing.

TARRAGON CHICKEN

Chicken can be crumbed 2 days ahead; keep, covered, in refrigerator or freeze for 3 months. Recipe unsuitable to microwave.

4 chicken breast fillets
plain flour
1 egg, lightly beaten
1½ cups (150g) stale breadcrumbs
oil for deep-frying
TARRAGON BUTTER
125g butter
2 teaspoons chopped fresh tarragon
2 teaspoons canned drained green peppercorns, crushed
1 tablespoon grated parmesan cheese

Cut fillets in half crossways. Lightly pound each piece until thin, top with a tarragon butter log; roll up to enclose butter securely.

Toss rolls in flour; shake away excess flour. Dip rolls in egg, then toss in breadcrumbs. Place rolls on tray, refrigerate for 30 minutes. Deep-fry rolls in batches in hot oil, for about 5 minutes or until golden brown. Drain on absorbent paper.

Tarragon Butter: Cream butter, tarragon, peppercorns and cheese in small bowl until combined. Divide mixture into 8 portions, place each portion onto foil, shape into thin log, wrap in foil, twisting ends firmly; refrigerate until firm.

Serves 4.

LEFT: Tarragon Chicken.

Left: Plate, board and garlic: The Country Trader; cabinet: Flossoms; linen: Accoutrement

KUMARA SOUFFLES WITH CREAMY TARRAGON SAUCE

Kumara is an orange-coloured sweet potato. Make soufflés just before serving. Sauce can be made several hours ahead; keep, covered, in refrigerator. Recipe unsuitable to freeze or microwave.

⅓ cup packaged breadcrumbs
400g kumara, chopped
⅓ cup sour cream
**2 tablespoons grated fresh
  parmesan cheese**
1 teaspoon grated lemon rind
¼ teaspoon ground nutmeg
4 eggs, separated
CREAMY TARRAGON SAUCE
1 cup cream
**2 tablespoons chopped fresh
  tarragon**
2 teaspoons seeded mustard
1 teaspoon cornflour
2 teaspoons lemon juice

Grease 4 soufflé dishes (1 cup capacity), sprinkle inside dishes with breadcrumbs; shake away excess breadcrumbs.

Boil, steam or microwave kumara until tender; drain. Process kumara, sour cream, cheese, rind, nutmeg and egg yolks until smooth. Transfer mixture to large bowl. Beat egg whites in medium bowl until firm peaks form, fold into kumara mixture. Spoon mixture into prepared dishes, bake in moderately hot oven for about 20 minutes or until puffed and golden brown. Serve immediately with sauce.

Creamy Tarragon Sauce: Combine cream, tarragon and mustard in small saucepan. Blend cornflour with juice, stir into cream mixture, stir over high heat until sauce boils and thickens.

Serves 4.

TARRAGON VINEGAR

Vinegar will keep in jars in a cool dark place for 3 months. Recipe unsuitable to freeze.

1 litre (4 cups) white wine vinegar
10 sprigs fresh tarragon
10 whole black peppercorns
3 cloves garlic, peeled

Combine vinegar, half the tarragon, peppercorns and garlic in large bowl, cover, stand overnight in a warm place or until tarragon loses colour; strain. Place remaining tarragon in jars, top with vinegar.

Makes 1 litre (4 cups).

TOP LEFT: Kumara Soufflés with Creamy Tarragon Sauce. LEFT: Tarragon Vinegar.

Top left: Soufflé dishes: Accoutrement; spoon: Appley Hoare Antiques; duck and fabric: Decorator Blinds. Left: Tiles: Old Balgowlah Restorations

PEPPER TARRAGON STEAKS

Recipe is best made close to serving time. Recipe unsuitable to freeze or microwave.

45g butter
1 tablespoon oil
1 clove garlic, crushed
4 thick Scotch fillet steaks
2 tablespoons plain flour
¼ cup dry sherry
1 cup water
2 small beef stock cubes, crumbled
¼ cup orange juice

1 tablespoon canned drained green
    peppercorns
1 teaspoon French mustard
2 tablespoons chopped fresh
    tarragon
½ cup cream

Heat butter and oil in large frying pan, add garlic, stir over medium heat for 1 minute. Add steaks, cook over high heat for about 2 minutes on each side or until well browned and tender. Remove from pan, keep warm.

Add flour to pan, stir over medium heat for 1 minute. Remove from heat, gradually stir in combined sherry, water, stock cubes, juice and peppercorns, stir over high heat until mixture boils and thickens; stir in mustard. Reduce heat, stir in tarragon and cream. Serve sauce with steaks.

Serves 4.

ABOVE: Pepper Tarragon Steaks.

Basket: The Country Trader.

113

CHICKEN SALAD WITH TARRAGON AND COCONUT

We used peanut oil for the dressing. Salad and dressing can be made a day ahead; keep, covered, in refrigerator. Recipe unsuitable to freeze.

No. 12 barbecued chicken
3 bacon rashers, chopped
1 small red Spanish onion, chopped
1 medium avocado, chopped
250g punnet cherry tomatoes
1 small green cucumber, chopped
⅓ cup stuffed green olives, halved
1 cos lettuce
TARRAGON COCONUT DRESSING
1 teaspoon chopped fresh tarragon
3 teaspoons tomato paste
2 teaspoons sambal oelek
½ teaspoon sugar
¼ cup coconut cream
⅓ cup oil

Remove skin and bones from chicken; chop chicken. Cook bacon in small frying pan over medium heat until lightly browned; drain on absorbent paper.

Combine chicken, bacon, onion, avocado, tomatoes, cucumber and olives in large bowl. Place lettuce in bowl, top with chicken mixture. Pour dressing over salad just before serving.

Tarragon Coconut Dressing: Blend or process tarragon, paste, sambal oelek, sugar and cream until combined. With motor operating, gradually add oil in a thin stream, blend until mixture is thick.

Serves 6.

MARINATED OCTOPUS SALAD

Salad can be made 2 days ahead; keep, covered, in refrigerator. Recipe unsuitable to freeze or microwave.

1kg baby octopus
3 cups dry white wine
3 cups water
2 sprigs fresh tarragon
2 sprigs fresh thyme
2 bay leaves

1 tablespoon canned drained green peppercorns
DRESSING
¼ cup oil
2 tablespoons olive oil
¼ cup lemon juice
1 clove garlic, crushed
1 tablespoon chopped fresh tarragon

Remove and discard heads from octopus, cut octopus in half. Combine octopus, wine, water, tarragon, thyme, bay leaves and peppercorns in large saucepan, bring to boil, reduce heat, cover, simmer for about 45 minutes or until octopus are tender. Drain octopus, place in large bowl; cool. Pour dressing over octopus, mix well, cover, refrigerate overnight.

Dressing: Combine all ingredients in jar, shake well.

Serves 4.

ABOVE: Marinated Octopus Salad. RIGHT: Chicken Salad with Tarragon and Coconut.

THYME

The small, pointed grey leaves of garden thyme (Thymus vulgaris) have a pungent aroma and a warm, herby taste. Its name comes from the Greek, meaning "to fumigate", and it was used in those times as a temple incense.

Oil of thyme (thymol) is contained in many modern-day cough mixtures, and is an ingredient in the liqueur, Benedictine. Thyme is a vital part of New Orleans Creole cooking, and goes well with soups, stews, stuffings, pâtés, herb bread and vegetables.

ABOVE RIGHT: Feta Cheese in Herb Oil.
RIGHT: Warm Marinated Fish with Vegetables.

Above right: Stool: Country Form

FETA CHEESE IN HERB OIL

Recipe can be made a week ahead; keep, covered, in cool dark place. Recipe unsuitable to freeze.

500g block feta cheese
1½ cups milk
1½ cups water
3 sprigs fresh thyme
2 sprigs fresh rosemary
3 small fresh red chillies
2 cloves garlic, peeled
1 tablespoon yellow mustard seeds
2 teaspoons fennel seeds
2 teaspoons dried juniper berries
4 bay leaves
1 teaspoon grated lemon rind
2 cups olive oil, approximately

Cut cheese into 3cm slices, place into large bowl with milk and water, cover, refrigerate overnight; drain. Arrange cheese, thyme, rosemary, chillies, garlic, seeds, berries, bay leaves and rind in large jar, cover with oil. Serve with crusty bread.

WARM MARINATED FISH WITH VEGETABLES

Recipe can be prepared a day ahead; keep, covered, in refrigerator. You will need about 6 limes for this recipe. We used snapper fillets in this recipe. This recipe is unsuitable to freeze or microwave.

1 large red pepper
1 large green pepper
1 medium eggplant, chopped
2 spring onions, thinly sliced
500g white fish fillets, skinned, sliced
MARINADE
1 tablespoon fresh chopped flat-leafed parsley
2 tablespoons chopped fresh thyme
¼ teaspoon ground cinnamon
1 tablespoon dry red wine
1 teaspoon sugar
½ cup olive oil
½ cup water
½ cup lime juice

Cut peppers into quarters lengthways, remove seeds and membranes; place skin-side-up in single layer on oven tray, grill until skins blister. Wrap peppers in a clean cloth, stand for 5 minutes, peel away skin. Cut peppers into strips.

Combine peppers, eggplant, onions and fish in medium bowl, stir in marinade, cover, refrigerate overnight. Add mixture to large frying pan or wok, stir gently over medium heat until heated through.

Marinade: Combine all ingredients in jar, shake well.

Serves 4.

THYME, PRAWN AND MUSTARD SOUP

Soup is best made just before serving. Recipe unsuitable to freeze.

60g butter
8 green shallots, chopped
¼ cup plain flour
3 cups water
2 small chicken stock cubes,
** crumbled**
¼ cup dry white wine
2 teaspoons French mustard
1 tablespoon tomato paste
2 teaspoons chopped fresh thyme
500g uncooked king prawns, shelled
¾ cup cream

Melt butter in large saucepan, add shallots, stir over medium heat for about 2 minutes (or microwave on HIGH for about 2 minutes) or until shallots are soft. Stir in flour, stir over medium heat for 2 minutes (or microwave on HIGH for 1 minute).

Remove from heat, gradually stir in combined water, stock cubes, wine, mustard, paste and thyme. Stir over high heat (or microwave on HIGH for about 5 minutes) until mixture boils and thickens.

Stir in prawns and cream, reduce heat, simmer, uncovered, for about 5 minutes (or microwave on HIGH for about 5 minutes) or until prawns are tender.

Serves 4.

PASTA WITH MUSHROOM CREAM

Recipe is best made just before serving. We used fresh fettucine in this recipe; you can substitute 400g dried fettucine. Recipe unsuitable to freeze or microwave.

60g butter
1 medium onion, chopped
500g large mushrooms, sliced
300ml carton thickened cream
1 small chicken stock cube,
** crumbled**
1 teaspoon seeded mustard
1 tablespoon sprigs fresh thyme
750g fresh tomato pasta

Melt butter in medium frying pan, add onion, stir over medium heat for about 2 minutes or until onion is soft. Add mushrooms, gently stir over medium heat for about 4 minutes or until mushrooms are tender. Stir in cream, stock cube and mustard, bring to boil, reduce heat, simmer, uncovered, for about 5 minutes, stir in thyme just before serving. Sprinkle with extra thyme, if desired.

Add pasta gradually to large saucepan of boiling water, boil, uncovered, until just tender, drain. Serve sauce over pasta.

Serves 4.

THYME SEASONED GARFISH WITH PEACH SALSA

Garfish can be prepared several hours ahead; keep, covered, in refrigerator. Garfish are best cooked close to serving time. Peach salsa can be made several hours ahead; keep, covered, in refrigerator. Recipe unsuitable to freeze or microwave.

8 medium garfish
plain flour
1 egg, lightly beaten
1 tablespoon milk
1 cup stale white breadcrumbs
oil for shallow-frying
THYME SEASONING
90g packaged cream cheese,
softened
½ cup grated Jarlsberg or Swiss
cheese
1½ tablespoons chopped
fresh thyme
1 tablespoon lemon juice
few drops tabasco sauce
PEACH SALSA
2 tablespoons oil
1 medium onion, chopped
1 small fresh green chilli, chopped
1 tablespoon lemon juice
1 medium peach, chopped

Remove heads and backbones from garfish. Place 4 garfish skin-side-down on bench, spread with thyme seasoning, top with remaining garfish; press together firmly. Toss garfish lightly in flour; shake away excess flour. Dip garfish into combined egg and milk, then in breadcrumbs; press crumbs on firmly.

Shallow-fry garfish in hot oil for about 3 minutes on each side or until fish are tender. Drain on absorbent paper, serve with peach salsa.

Thyme Seasoning: Combine all ingredients in medium bowl; mix well.

Peach Salsa: Heat oil in small saucepan, add onion, chilli and juice, cover, cook over low heat for about 30 minutes, stirring occasionally. Stir in peach.

Serves 4.

TOP LEFT: Thyme, Prawn and Mustard Soup. BELOW LEFT: Pasta with Mushroom Cream. BELOW: Thyme Seasoned Garfish with Peach Salsa.

Below left: Plate and bowl: Village Living

CHICKEN WITH THYME BUTTER SAUCE

Chicken is best prepared close to serving time. This recipe is unsuitable to freeze.

4 chicken breast fillets
plain flour
¼ cup olive oil
125g butter
1 tablespoon chopped fresh thyme
2 green shallots, chopped
¼ cup lemon juice

Toss chicken in flour, shake away excess flour. Heat oil and half the butter in large frying pan, add chicken to pan, cook over medium heat for about 10 minutes (or microwave on HIGH for about 8 minutes) or until chicken is tender. Drain chicken on absorbent paper, keep warm. Discard pan juices.

Heat remaining butter in same pan, add thyme and shallots, stir over medium heat for about 2 minutes (or microwave on HIGH for about 2 minutes) or until shallots are soft. Stir in juice, cook over medium heat for 3 minutes (or microwave on HIGH for 3 minutes). Serve over chicken.

Serves 4.

LOBSTER WITH THYME AND DRAMBUIE SAUCE

Lobster is best cooked close to serving time. Sauce can be made 2 days ahead; keep, covered, in refrigerator. Drambuie is a liqueur based on whisky, flavoured with herbs and honey.

4 small uncooked lobster tails
45g butter
THYME AND DRAMBUIE SAUCE
15g butter
2 green shallots, chopped
3 teaspoons chopped fresh thyme
2 tablespoons Drambuie
1 cup cream
1 teaspoon plain flour

1 teaspoon butter, extra

Cut lobster tails in half lengthways. Melt butter in large frying pan, add tails, flesh side down, cover, cook over medium heat for about 10 minutes or until tender. Serve with sauce.

Thyme and Drambuie Sauce: Melt butter in medium saucepan, add shallots and thyme, stir over medium heat for about 1 minute (or microwave on HIGH for about 2 minutes) or until shallots are soft. Stir in liqueur and cream, bring to boil, reduce heat, simmer for 1 minute (or microwave on HIGH for 2 minutes). Stir in combined flour and extra butter, stir over medium heat (or microwave on HIGH for about 2 minutes) until mixture boils and thickens; strain before serving.

Serves 4.

ABOVE: Chicken with Thyme Butter Sauce. RIGHT: Lobster with Thyme and Drambuie Sauce.

Above: Plate: The Country Trader; cutlery: Made Where

WATERCRESS

Watercress (Nasturtium officinale) grows in running water, on river banks or in regularly watered tubs and moist shady positions. It has a sharp peppery flavour and is fresh and tangy to taste. It has been described in an early Anglo-Saxon herbal as a sacred herb, used to repel evil. Watercress adds a hot spiciness to salads and sandwiches. The chopped leaves can be mixed with mayonnaise to make a savoury dip.

WATERCRESS SALAD WITH SESAME DRESSING

Salad is best prepared close to serving time. Recipe unsuitable to freeze or microwave.

1 medium tomato, peeled, chopped
2 green shallots, chopped
1 medium red pepper, chopped
1 medium avocado, chopped
1 small green cucumber, chopped
2 cups fresh watercress

SESAME DRESSING
2 tablespoons sweet chilli sauce
½ cup oil
½ teaspoon light soy sauce
¼ teaspoon sesame oil
2 tablespoons cider vinegar
2 tablespoons lemon juice
1 teaspoon sugar
¼ cup sesame seeds

Combine tomato, shallots, pepper, avocado and cucumber in medium bowl, add dressing; mix well. Place watercress on plate, top with salad.

Sesame Dressing: Combine all ingredients in small bowl; mix well.

Serves 4.

MOULDED CRESS SALAD

Recipe is best made a day ahead; keep, covered, in refrigerator. This recipe is unsuitable to freeze or microwave.

2 tablespoons gelatine
1 cup water
2 small beef stock cubes, crumbled
250g packet cream cheese
½ cup mayonnaise
1 cup plain yoghurt
¼ cup dry sherry
1 teaspoon cracked black
  peppercorns
1 tablespoon grated lemon rind
¼ cup chopped fresh watercress
1 large carrot, finely grated
1 large (200g) zucchini, finely grated

Sprinkle gelatine over combined water and stock cubes in small bowl, stand in small pan of simmering water, stir until dissolved (or microwave on HIGH for 1½ minutes); cool slightly.

Beat cheese, mayonnaise and yoghurt in medium bowl with electric mixer until smooth. Stir in sherry, peppercorns, rind, watercress and gelatine mixture.

Pour one-third of the cheese mixture into lightly oiled ring mould (6 cup capacity); refrigerate until set.

Spoon carrot into mould, leaving about 1cm border at outer and inner edges of mould. Spread with half the remaining cheese mixture, filling in borders around the carrot; refrigerate until set.

Squeeze excess moisture from zucchini, spoon zucchini into mould, leaving about 2cm border at outer and inner edges of mould. Spread with remaining cheese mixture, filling in

borders around zucchini; refrigerate until set. Turn mould onto plate, cut into slices, serve with extra watercress, if desired.

Serves 8.

LOIN OF LAMB WITH WATERCRESS SEASONING

Ask your butcher to bone the lamb for you. Lamb can be prepared a day ahead; keep, covered, in refrigerator. Recipe unsuitable to freeze. Lamb and sauce unsuitable to microwave.

1½kg loin of lamb, boned
1 tablespoon oil
1 clove garlic, crushed
2 teaspoons chopped fresh
**   rosemary**
WATERCRESS SEASONING
¾ cup cracked wheat
15g butter
2 cloves garlic, crushed
1 small red pepper, finely chopped
½ cup stale breadcrumbs
1 small tomato, peeled, chopped
1 cup chopped fresh watercress
WATERCRESS BEARNAISE
¼ cup tarragon vinegar
2 green shallots, chopped
2 egg yolks
125g butter, melted
¼ cup fresh watercress

Spread lamb on bench, fat side down. Spread seasoning over lamb flap, roll lamb tightly, secure with string at 5cm intervals. Brush lamb with combined oil, garlic and rosemary, place lamb in baking dish, bake in moderate oven for about 1¼ hours or until cooked as desired. Serve hot or cold with sauce.

Watercress Seasoning: Place wheat in small bowl, cover with boiling water, stand for 15 minutes. Drain wheat, pat dry with absorbent paper.

Melt butter in small saucepan, add garlic and pepper, stir over medium heat for about 2 minutes (or microwave on HIGH for about 2 minutes) or until pepper is soft, cool. Combine wheat, breadcrumbs, pepper mixture, tomato and watercress in large bowl; mix well.

Watercress Bearnaise: Combine vinegar and shallots in small saucepan, bring to boil, reduce heat, simmer, uncovered, until reduced to about 2 tablespoons, strain; cool. Blend or process egg yolks and vinegar until smooth, gradually pour in hot bubbling butter while motor is operating. Stir in watercress.

Serves 4.

LEFT: Watercress Salad with Sesame Dressing. ABOVE RIGHT: Moulded Cress Salad. RIGHT: Loin of Lamb with Watercress Seasoning.

Right: Plate: Mikasa

HOW TO DRY HERBS

When you have an abundance of fresh herbs, you can easily dry them and keep them for future use.

AIR DRYING

Most fresh herbs can be air dried and then stored in air-tight, screw-top containers, preferably glass jars.

It is always best to pick the herbs in the morning, when the dew has dried but before the sun has been on them for too long. Large leaves should be separated from their stalks, small leaves can be left on and rubbed off after drying.

Spread the clean leaves or leaf-bearing stalks in a single layer on a piece of gauze or insect screen stretched across a frame and supported so the air can circulate freely underneath; put the frame in a dark, warm, dry place. Depending upon the weather conditions, the leaves should become crisp and dry within about a week. Avoid drying herbs in damp or humid weather.

An alternate way to dry herbs is to tie them up in decorative bunches and hang them in a well-aired place to dry, away from direct light. This method is recommended for large, thick leaves such as bay leaves.

MICROWAVING

You can successfully dry herbs, grown at home or purchased from the fruit and vegetable shop, in a microwave oven.

A certain amount of trial and error is involved with this method, as the power output of microwave ovens varies, as does the moisture content of the herbs you wish to dry.

The first step is to spread the clean, dry leaves in a single layer on 3 folds of absorbent paper in the microwave oven, then cook for 2 minutes on HIGH.

When the 2 minutes are up, feel the leaves and remove any that are crisp. Repeat this procedure with all the remaining leaves; however, this time turning them over and checking them for crispness every 30 seconds. Continue to remove the crisp leaves until the few that remain cover about 4 square centimetres of absorbent paper. The small amount of remaining leaves can be discarded or allowed to air dry.

STORAGE

Whichever method of drying you have used, always store the herbs in air-tight, screw-top glass jars and check for crispness and aroma at least once a month. Discard if there is any indication of mould, as this is a sign that the leaves were not dry enough when stored, or that they have absorbed moisture after drying.

KEY
1. Sage **2.** Marjoram **3.** Tarragon **4.** Sage
5. Lemon Grass **6.** Oregano **7.** Variety
8. Garlic **9.** Chervil **10.** Chives
11. Bergamot **12.** Basil **13.** Mint
14. Rosemary **15.** Thyme **16.** Coriander
17. Bay Leaves **18.** Chilli

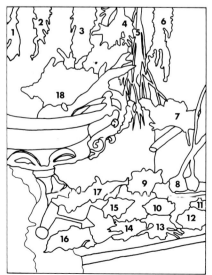

GLOSSARY

Some terms, names and alternatives are included here to help everyone to understand and use our recipes.

Allspice: pimento in ground form.

Bacon Rashers: bacon slices.

Baking Powder: is a raising agent consisting of an alkali and acid. It is mostly made from cream of tartar and bicarbonate of soda in the proportion of 1 level teaspoon cream of tartar to ½ level teaspoon bicarbonate of soda. This is equivalent to 2 teaspoons baking powder.

Bicarbonate of soda: baking soda.

Bocconcini: small balls of mild, delicate cheese packaged in water or whey to keep them white and soft. The water should be just milky in appearance and cheese should be white; yellowing indicates that it is too old.

Breadcrumbs: *Stale:* use 1 or 2 day old white bread made into crumbs by grating, blending or processing. *Packaged:* use commercially packaged breadcrumbs.

Butter: we used salted and unsalted (sweet) butter in this book; 125g butter equals 1 stick butter.

Buttermilk: the liquid left after cream is separated from milk. It is slightly sour in taste; use skim milk if unavailable.

Chick Pea Flour: made from ground chick peas. Also known as gram or besan flour.

Chick Peas: also known as garbanzos, when canned. They are a staple food in the Middle East and are available from supermarkets and health food shops.

Chillies: fresh and dried; are available in many different types and sizes. The small ones (bird's eye or bird pepper) are the hottest. Use tight-fitting gloves when chopping fresh chillies as they can burn your skin. The seeds are the hottest part of the chillies, so remove them if you want to reduce the heat content of recipes.

Cider Vinegar: vinegar made from fermented apples.

Coconut Cream: available in cans and cartons in supermarkets and Asian stores; coconut milk can be substituted although it is not as thick.

Cooking Salt: a coarse salt (not the same as fine table salt).

Cornflour: cornstarch.

Couscous: a cereal processed into tiny grains from semolina.

Cracked Wheat: processed wheat of Mediterranean and Middle Eastern origin; also known as burghul or bulgur.

Cream: *Thickened (whipping) cream:* is specified when necessary in recipes. *Cream:* is simply a light pouring cream, also known as half 'n' half. *Sour:* a thick commercially cultured soured cream. *Sour light:* a less dense commercially cultured sour cream.

Dried Herbs: we used dried (not ground herbs) in the proportion of 1:4 for fresh herbs; for example, 1 teaspoon dried herbs instead of 4 teaspoons (1 tablespoon) chopped fresh herbs.

Drumsticks: section cut from the first joint on a chicken leg.

Eggplant: aubergine.

Fish Sauce: is an essential ingredient in the cooking of a number of Asian countries including Thailand and Vietnam. It is made from the liquid drained from salted, fermented anchovies. The amount you add to recipes depends on personal taste.

Flour: *Plain flour:* all-purpose flour. *Self-raising flour:* substitute plain (all-purpose) flour and baking powder in the proportion of ¾ metric cup plain flour to 2 level metric teaspoons baking powder; sift together several times. If using an 8oz measuring cup, use 1 cup plain flour to 2 level metric teaspoons baking powder. *Wholemeal:* wholegrain flour; see self-raising flour and baking powder proportions for how to make wholemeal self-raising flour.

Fontina Cheese: is Italian in origin and has a brown or red rind. It is semi-hard with a nutty flavour and a few holes.

Garam Masala: there are many variations of the combinations of cardamom, cinnamon, cloves, coriander, cumin and nutmeg used to make up this spice used often in Indian cooking. Sometimes pepper is used to make a hot variation. Garam masala is readily available in jars from Asian food stores and supermarkets.

Gherkin: cornichon.

Glace Ginger: fresh ginger which has been boiled and preserved in sugar syrup.

Green Ginger Wine: wine flavoured with fresh ginger; mainly used in cooking and cocktails. This wine has an alcohol content around 16%.

Green Peppercorns: canned, fresh peppercorns in brine.

Hoisin Sauce: a thick sweet Chinese barbecue sauce made from salted black beans, onions and garlic.

Juniper Berries: dried berries of an evergreen tree; it is the main flavouring ingredient in gin.

Kiwi Fruit (Chinese Gooseberry): fruit with hairy skin and soft, sweet green-coloured flesh. The skin can be eaten.

Lamb Fillets: a very small, tender cut of meat found between the loin and chump.

Lamb's Fry: lamb's liver.

Lavash Bread: flat, unleavened bread of Mediterranean origin.

Lentils: there are many different types of lentils; they require overnight soaking before cooking (the exception is red lentils (orange in colour), which are ready for cooking without soaking).

Lettuce: we used mostly iceberg, radicchio, mignonette, cos and butter lettuce in our recipes.

Lobster: crayfish.

Madeira: wine fortified with brandy.

Maple Syrup: golden/pancake syrup; honey can be substituted.

Minced Beef: ground beef.

Mustard, Seeded: a French-style of textured mustard with crushed mustard seeds.

Oil: we used light polyunsaturated salad oil in our recipes unless otherwise stated.

Olive Oil: virgin oil is obtained only from the pulp of high-grade fruit. Pure olive oil is pressed from the pulp and kernels of second grade olives.

Oyster Sauce: a rich brown sauce made from oysters cooked in salt and soy sauce, then thickened with different starches.

Peppers: capsicum or bell peppers.

Pimento: allspice.

Pimientos: sweet red peppers preserved in brine in cans or jars.

Pita Bread: pocket bread.

Prosciutto: uncooked, unsmoked ham cured in salt, usually bought in very thin slices; it is ready to eat when bought.

Punnet: basket holding about 250g fruit.

Rockmelon: cantaloupe.

Sambal Oelek: (also spelt sambal uelek); a paste made from ground chillies and salt, used as an ingredient or an accompaniment.

Scotch Fillet: basic cut of beef from the rib area.

Sesame Oil: is an aromatic oil with a nutty flavour made from toasted, crushed, white sesame seeds. It is always used in small quantities, and added mostly towards the end of cooking time. It should not be used to fry food, but as a flavouring only. It can be bought in supermarkets and Asian food stores; store in refrigerator.

Shallots: *golden shallots:* a member of the onion family, with a delicate onion/garlic flavour; *green shallots:* known as spring onions in some Australian states; scallions in some other countries.

Smoked Cod Roe: eggs of cod fish which have been smoked.

Snow Peas: (also known as mange tout, sugar peas or Chinese peas). The small flat pods and tiny, barely formed peas inside are eaten whole — pod and all. They require only a short cooking time (about 30 seconds) either by stir-frying or blanching. Top and tail, if desired.

Soy Sauce: made from fermented soy beans; we used 2 types, the light and dark variety. The light sauce is generally used with white meat dishes, and the darker variety with red meat dishes, but this is only a guide. Dark soy is generally used for colour, and the light soy for flavour. Light soy sauce has more salt than dark.

Sprouts: the bean sprouts used in this book are mung bean sprouts; these should be topped and tailed. Newly sprouted mung beans are only tiny — about 3cm long — and usually have the green outer husk intact. These are the simplest beans to sprout at home. There are many varieties of sprouts; they can all be substituted for each other. Adjust cooking times to allow for shorter cooking for the finer sprouts like alfalfa.

Stock Cube: a small cube is equivalent to 1 teaspoon powdered bouillon, large cube is equivalent to 2 teaspoons bouillon. They have a high salt content.

Sugar: *Brown:* soft, fine, brown sugar. ***Castor:*** fine granulated table sugar. ***Crystal:*** coarse granulated table sugar. ***Icing:*** confectioners' or powdered sugar.

Sugar Snap Peas: are small pods with small formed peas inside; they are eaten whole, cooked or uncooked. They require only a short cooking time.

Sun-Dried Tomatoes: are dried tomatoes sometimes bottled in oil.

Sweet Chilli Sauce: it consists of chillies, salt, sugar and vinegar. We used it sparingly so that you can easily increase amounts in recipes to suit your taste.

Tamarind Sauce: is made from the acid-tasting fruit of the tamarind tree. If unavailable, soak about 30g dried tamarind in a cup of water, stand for 10 minutes. Squeeze the pulp as dry as possible and use the flavoured water.

Tomato Purée: known as tomato sauce in some countries. You can use canned tomato purée or purée of fresh ripe tomatoes made by blending or processing the amount required.

Tomato Sauce: tomato ketchup.

White Wine Vinegar: made from white wine, flavoured with herbs, spices, fruit.

Wine: we used good quality dry white and red wines.

Wholemeal Flour: wholegrain flour.

Yeast: allow 3 teaspoons (7g) dried granulated yeast to 15g compressed yeast.

Yoghurt: plain, unflavoured yoghurt used as a meat tenderiser, enricher, thickener and also as a dessert ingredient.

Zucchini: courgette.

OVEN TEMPERATURES

Electric Temperatures	Celsius	Fahrenheit	Gas Temperatures	Celsius	Fahrenheit
Very slow	120	250	Very slow	120	250
Slow	150	300	Slow	150	300
Moderately slow	160-180	325-350	Moderately slow	160	325
Moderate	180-200	375-400	Moderate	180	350
Moderately hot	210-230	425-450	Moderately hot	190	375
Hot	240-250	475-500	Hot	200	400
Very hot	260	525-550	Very hot	230	450

CUP AND SPOON MEASURES

Recipes in this book use this standard metric equipment approved by the Australian Standards Association:

(a) 250 millilitre cup for measuring liquids. A litre jug (capacity 4 cups) is also available.

(b) a graduated set of four cups — measuring 1 cup, half, third and quarter cup — for items such as flour, sugar, etc. When measuring in these fractional cups, level off at the brim.

(c) a graduated set of four spoons: tablespoon (20 millilitre liquid capacity), teaspoon (5 millilitre), half and quarter teaspoons. The Australian, British and American teaspoon each has 5ml capacity.

All spoon measurements are level.
Note: We have used large eggs with an average weight of 61g each in all recipes.

APPROXIMATE CUP AND SPOON CONVERSION CHART

Australian	American & British	Australian	American & British
1 cup	1¼ cups	⅓ cup	½ cup
¾ cup	1 cup	¼ cup	⅓ cup
⅔ cup	¾ cup	2 tablespoons	¼ cup
½ cup	⅔ cup	1 tablespoon	3 teaspoons

INDEX